What readers are saying about *Pragmatic Data Crunching*

This book is full of useful practical tips; even more important, it distills a lifetime's worth of real-life experience about the kinds of everyday, down-to-earth data manipulation issues that hardly anybody writes about. It's the next-best thing to having twenty years' experience in programming and data handling.

▶ **Alex Martelli**
Author, *Python in a Nutshell*

Greg has done a wonderful job of bringing together a much-needed essay of techniques, tips, and tricks on data manipulation. His examples are current and his humor enjoyable. I recommend you get a copy of this book if you are embarking on a journey that involves working among differing data formats.

▶ **Brent Gorda**

I wish I had read this book or its equivalent about fifteen years ago.

▶ **Michelle Wahl Craig**
Faculty, University of Toronto

A very pleasant read. It covers the core concepts with just enough background information to prevent it from sounding like a beginner's handbook.

▶ **Jason Montojo**
Blueprint

Overall, a nice short book, covering important topics in a reasonable level of depth and breadth. Nice job. I'd certainly recommend it.

▶ **David Ascher**
ActiveState

Data Crunching

Solve Everyday Problems Using Java, Python, and More

Data Crunching

Solve Everyday Problems Using Java, Python, and More

Greg Wilson

The Pragmatic Bookshelf
Raleigh, North Carolina   Dallas, Texas

Many of the designations used by manufacturers and sellers to distinguish their products are claimed as trademarks. Where those designations appear in this book, and The Pragmatic Programmers, LLC was aware of a trademark claim, the designations have been printed in initial capital letters or in all capitals. The Pragmatic Starter Kit, The Pragmatic Programmer, Pragmatic Programming, Pragmatic Bookshelf and the linking *g* device are trademarks of The Pragmatic Programmers, LLC.

Every precaution was taken in the preparation of this book. However, the publisher assumes no responsibility for errors or omissions, or for damages that may result from the use of information (including program listings) contained herein.

Our Pragmatic courses, workshops, and other products can help you and your team create better software and have more fun. For more information, as well as the latest Pragmatic titles, please visit us at

    http://www.pragmaticprogrammer.com

ISBN 0-9745140-7-1

Printed on acid-free paper with 85% recycled, 30% post-consumer content.

First printing, April 2005

Version: 2005-3-22

Contents

Chapter 1

Introduction

A friend of mine used to have a sign over his desk that said, "The first 90% of the work takes the first 90% of the time. The other 10% of the work takes the other 90% of the time." If you're a programmer, some of that "other 90%" is probably spent crunching data. This book will show you how to do it faster and how to get it right on the first try.

So what exactly is *data crunching*? The easiest way to explain is with a couple of stories....

1.1   Name That Molecule

A few years ago, when 3D graphics cards were still a novelty on PCs, a high school science teacher asked me to help her create images of various molecules. In one hand, she had some files that specified the coordinates of the atoms in water, ethanol, caffeine, and other compounds. Each file was in PDB (Protein Data Bank) format and looked something like this:

```
COMPND        Ammonia
AUTHOR        DAVE WOODCOCK  97 10 31
ATOM      1  N           1      0.257   -0.363    0.000
ATOM      2  H           1      0.257    0.727    0.000
ATOM      3  H           1      0.771   -0.727    0.890
ATOM      4  H           1      0.771   -0.727   -0.890
TER       5              1
END
```

In the other hand, she had a Fortran program that could draw spheres. Its input had to be in a format called VU3, which looked like this:

```
-- Nitrogen
1 17 0.5 0.257 -0.363 0.000
-- Hydrogens
1 6 0.2 0.257 0.727 0.000
1 6 0.2 0.771 -0.727 0.890
1 6 0.2 0.771 -0.727 -0.890
```

Each line represents a single object. "1" means "sphere"; "17" is the color code for purple, "6" for gray, and the other numbers are the sphere's radius and XYZ coordinates.

Translating the file for ammonia from PDB to VU3 took about thirty seconds using Notepad. At that rate, translating the file for cholesterol (which has 78 atoms) would have taken several minutes; fixing the typos that would inevitably creep in would probably have taken a few minutes more, and we would still have the other 100-plus molecules to deal with.

Data crunching to the rescue. What we needed was a program that would do the translations for us. We didn't really care how fast it ran, but it had to be easy to write (or else it would have been more economical for my friend to assign the translation of the molecule data to her students as homework).

It took me about three minutes to write a program to do the job and another couple of minutes to find and fix two bugs in it. Translating 112 molecules then took less than a minute. A month later, when my friend switched graphics programs, it took her only a couple of minutes to modify the code to generate the files the new program needed. Ten minutes of programming saved her and her students several hours of tedious typing.

1.2 There's One in Every Crowd...

A few years later, I was teaching a programming class at the University of Toronto. Five graduate students had been hired to mark my students' first assignment. Four of them submitted their grades via a web form, which created a file that looked like this:

```
<marks marker="Aliyah K." date="2003-09-27"
       course="csc207" exer="e1">
  <mark sid="g3allanj" grade="7.5"></mark>
  <mark sid="g3kowrem" grade="9.0"></mark>
  <mark sid="g3daniel" grade="2.0">Incomplete (no Makefile)</mark>
  ...
</marks>
```

The fifth marker—well, he must have had more important things to do than fill in HTML forms, because what I got from him was an email containing this:

```
g3andyh        6/10
g3davet        4/10      # More comments than code
g4mclark       2.5       # Infinite loop in part 3
  ...
```

Never mind the fact that it wasn't in XML—the grades themselves were written in two different ways. There were typos, too: all of the students' IDs should have started with *g3*, but he had some *g4*s and *f3*s in there as well.

When I bounced his message back to him, I got an autoreply saying that he was out of town for a conference and wouldn't be back for two weeks (which was long after marks were due). After adding a note to my calendar to chew him out, I saved his message to a file, edited it to strip off the mail headers, and started writing code. In less than two minutes, I was reading in his data; a minute after that, I had a list of all the student IDs in the file that *weren't* in the class list. It took a minute of editing to fix them and another minute to double-check my program's output, and I was done. It was five minutes I shouldn't have had to spend, but it was still a lot faster than anything else I could have done.

1.3 And the Moral Is...

On the face of it, Stone Age Fortran graphics and XML grade files don't have much in common. In both cases, though, a few simple techniques let me do things that would otherwise have been too time-consuming to be practical. All over the world, programmers use those same techniques every day to recycle legacy data, translate from one vendor's proprietary format into another's, check configuration files, and search through web logs to see how many people have downloaded the latest release of their product.

This kind of programming is usually called *data crunching* or *data munging*. These terms cover the tasks described above and dozens of others that are equally unglamorous but just as crucial.

There's no "grand unified theory" of data crunching, but a few fundamental patterns do crop up over and over again, regardless of what language the solution is written in or the exact details of the problem being solved. In this book, I'll show you what those patterns are, when you should use them, and how they'll make your life easier. Along the way, I'll introduce you to some handy, but underused, features of Java, Python, and other languages. I'll also show you how to test data crunching programs so that when it's *your* turn to reformat a file full of grades, you won't accidentally give someone a zero they don't deserve.

1.4 Questions About Data Crunching

Before diving into those patterns, I should probably answer three questions.

What Do You Need to Get Started?

In order to show you how to crunch data, this book has to show you examples, which have to be written in particular languages. I hope every example will be readable even if you haven't seen the language it's written in before (if it isn't, please let me know). If you want to try them out yourself, you'll need the following:

- A handful of classic Unix command-line tools. If you use Linux, Solaris, Mac OS X, or one of their cousins, you already have these. On Windows, you can install Cygwin, a collection of free-as-in-free software that is available at http://www.cygwin.com. Cygwin includes dozens of packages; you need only the defaults for this book, but you may find many of the others useful.

- Python. This is included by default in most Linux installations and in Mac OS X since release 10.3 (Panther); installers for other platforms are available at http://www.python.org. If you're using Windows, you might prefer the ActiveState installer, from http://www.activestate.com, which includes some useful Windows-specific extensions. I used Python 2.3 when writing this book, but any version from 2.2 onward will work just as well.

- Java. I believe that agile languages such as Python, Perl, and Ruby are the best way to tackle most data crunching problems. Since you may want to use a sturdy language, such as Java, C++, or C#,[1] I've included examples in Java to show you that the same ideas work with them just as well.

- A command-line XSLT processor. I used xsltproc, which is available in most Linux distributions and as part of Cygwin's libxml2 and libxslt packages.

- A relational database with a command-line interface. MySQL and PostgreSQL are the best-known names in the open source world, but I'm very fond of SQLite,[2] a small, lightweight system designed to be embedded directly into other programs. It isn't as fast as its bigger brothers and doesn't have nearly as many features, but setup is trivial, and its error messages are surprisingly helpful.

- Source code for the examples. You can download the source from the book's home page at www.pragmaticprogrammer.com/titles/gwd.

---

[1]For example, you might not be allowed to add another tool to the build environment, or it might be simpler to write your cruncher in C# than to figure out how to call a Python script from .NET.

[2]http://www.sqlite.org

> \\// **Joe Asks...**
> `~` **What About GUIs?**
>
> One thing you *won't* find in this book is any discussion of graphical interfaces. The reason is it's hard for other programs to read what GUIs produce. As you'll see over and over again in this book, data crunching tools are more effective in combination than they are on their own.
>
> That said, you can do a lot of sophisticated data crunching using GUI tools such as Microsoft Excel and OpenOffice Calc. Programmers (particularly Linux geeks) may sneer, but many accountants can do more in five minutes with Excel, Microsoft Access, and a little VB than most programmers can do in half an hour with their favorite programming language. A GUI is also a must when it comes time to display data to people—ASCII bar charts just don't cut it in the Twenty-First Century.

Is "Data Crunching" Just a Fancy Name for "Quick-and-Dirty Hacking"?

No. The fastest way to produce a working solution is always to program well. Even if you expect to run a piece of code only once, you should write meaningful comments, use sensible variable names, run a few tests, and do all of the other things Dave and Andy told you to do in [HT00]. Why? Because if you don't make a habit of doing those things all the time, every time, you won't do them the one time they would have saved you three hours of debugging, two hours before a deadline.

When Should I Use These Techniques?

The answer is simple: use these techniques whenever they'll save you time *in the long run.* If you want to copy ten numbers from one web site to another, the best thing to do is to open a second browser and start cutting and pasting. At the other end of the scale, if you have to move eighty million purchase records spread across eleven tables from an Oracle database into the CRM package your company just bought, then you have a full-blown software development project on your hands. The odds are pretty good that if you sit down and do some analysis and design, you'll have a working solution faster. What's more, whoever has to maintain your "one-time" solution will thank you, and you can never have too much good karma....

There's a lot of room between those two ends of the data processing spectrum and that's where these techniques come into their own. A typical situation is one in which:

- you can break the problem into simple transformations, each of which can be expressed in just a few lines;

- it's easy to check that your output is correct, so you don't need the kind of exhaustive unit testing you really should do in most cases;

- you're building a prototype of a more sophisticated solution (e.g., one element of a larger data processing pipeline that you'll replace as soon as Bob gets back from vacation and finishes what he was working on);

- enterprise-scale infrastructure support isn't an issue (i.e., you don't have to support your solution on hundreds or thousands of servers for several years); or

- your problem is I/O bound (i.e., the speed of your disk, your database, or your network dominates processing time), so a simple program will in practice run just as fast as a clever one.

1.5   Road Map

There's a lot of data out there crying out for crunching and a lot of different ways to crunch it. We'll cover the most common formats and techniques in the following order:

- Chapter 2, *Text*, on page 9: how to handle plain ol' text files and (more important) the general principles that underpin every well-behaved data crunching program.

- Chapter 3, *Regular Expressions*, on page 41: how to work with regular expressions, which are the power tools of text processing.

- Chapter 4, *XML*, on page 77: how to handle HTML and XML. We'll look at the three most common approaches: processing data as if it were a stream of tags, processing it as if it were a tree, and using a specialized language called XSLT.

- Chapter 5, *Binary Data*, on page 117: how to process binary data, such as images and ZIP files.

- Chapter 6, *Relational Databases*, on page 137: this is where data crunching blends into full-blown enterprise-scale data processing. I'll show you the

10% of SQL that will account for 90% of the queries you'll ever need to write, and warn you about a few common traps.

- Chapter 7, *Horseshoe Nails*, on page 167: a few topics that didn't fit elsewhere. The most important one is how to test data crunching programs, but I'll also cover some common data encoding schemes and how to handle dates and times.

Topics I *won't* cover are those specific to scientific number-crunching, particularly statistics and data visualization. As a one-time computational scientist, I think these are important, but they are complex enough to deserve a book of their own.

Acknowledgments

My name might be the only one on the spine of this book, but I had a lot of help writing it. In particular, I want to thank

- Brian Kernighan and his coauthors, for the books that taught my generation how to program ([KR98], [KP84], [KP81], and [KP78]);

- Irving Reid, Harald Koch, Gene Amdur, and the rest of the Select Access team, for teaching me the "other 90%" of software development;

- Prof. Diane Horton, and everyone else at the University of Toronto, for letting me put these ideas in front of impressionable young minds;

- Andy Hunt and Dave Thomas, for letting me talk them into this;

- the production team—Kim Wimpsett and Jim Moore—for turning electrons into pages;

- my wonderful reviewers (David Ascher, Michelle Craig, Elena Garderman, Steffen Gemkow, John Gilhuly, Brent Gorda, Adam Goucher, Mike Gunderloy, Alex Martelli, Jason Montojo, John Salama, Mike Stok, and Miles Thibault), without whom this book would be ful of misstakes;

- Sadie, for so much more than just homemade cornbread; and

- as always, my father, for teaching me how to write, and that writing well is important.

Chapter 2

Text

Line-oriented text is one of the oldest data formats around, and still one of the most popular. In part, it survives because most editors (including the one I'm using right now) display files as lines of text by default. A deeper reason is that it's very easy to write programs to manipulate text. In this chapter, we'll look at what those programs can do and how they should be structured. We'll also look at the Unix command line, a text-oriented programming environment that is still going strong after thirty-five years.

2.1 Reversing a File

Let's start with the "Hello, world" of data crunching: reversing the order of lines in a file. A simple Python solution is

```python
import sys

# Read
input = open(sys.argv[1], "r")
lines = input.readlines()
input.close()

# Process
lines.reverse()

# Write
output = open(sys.argv[2], "w")
for line in lines:
    print >> output, line.strip()
output.close()
```

It's almost trivial, but most data crunching programs follow the same pattern:

1. Read the input.
2. Process it.
3. Write the result.

In many cases, it's possible to write the output as we go along, but it's almost always a better idea to break the problem into the three discrete steps shown previously. For one thing, it makes it easier to reuse the reading and writing code (any file format you have to process once, you'll probably have to process again). For another, this approach works for every problem,[1] while there are many problems (such as reversing input) that print-as-you-go can't handle.

Now, if you prefer sturdy languages, you could write this Java program instead:

```java
import java.util.*;
import java.io.*;

public class ReverseLines {
  public static void main(String[] args) {
    try {
      // Read
      BufferedReader input = new BufferedReader(new FileReader(args[0]));
      ArrayList list = new ArrayList();
      String line;
      while ((line = input.readLine()) != null) {
        list.add(line);
      }
      input.close();

      // Process
      Collections.reverse(list);

      // Write
      PrintWriter output =
        new PrintWriter(new BufferedWriter(new FileWriter(args[1])));
      for (Iterator i=list.iterator(); i.hasNext(); ) {
        output.println((String)i.next());
      }
      output.close();
    }
    catch (IOException e) {
      System.err.println(e);
    }
  }
}
```

It's longer than its Python cousin, but they both do the same thing, in pretty much the same way.

Of course, a straight translation from one language to another usually doesn't produce the most natural, or most efficient, solution. A real Java programmer would put reading, processing, and writing in separate methods, would probably skip the call to reverse(), and iterate through the list in reverse order, like this:

```java
PrintWriter output =
    new PrintWriter(new BufferedWriter(new FileWriter(args[1])));
for (ListIterator i=list.listIterator(list.size()); i.hasPrevious(); ) {
    output.println((String)i.previous());
}
output.close();
```

---

[1]Unless the data set is so large that it won't fit into memory—a topic we'll return to later in this chapter.

What about error handling? What should the program do if the input file doesn't exist or if the output file can't be created? What if the output file already exists: should we overwrite it, prompt the user ("Destroy previous year's work: [y]es [n]o"), or print an error message and stop without doing anything? And what about handling multiple files at a time? Or merging files? Or solving the problem of world hunger, or getting Joss Whedon's *Firefly* back on the air?

These are all good questions, but they're about building applications, not about crunching data. If there's any realistic prospect that people you've never met will still be using the program you write after you've left the building, you should take a few minutes (at least) to think through these issues. If you're just trying to reformat an old data file so that your spreadsheet can read it, they aren't worth worrying about.

2.2 Reformatting Data

Let's revisit the problem of reformatting molecular data for 3D display. Each molecule is stored in a PDB file that looks something like this:

```
COMPND        Ammonia
AUTHOR        DAVE WOODCOCK  97 10 31
ATOM     1  N           1      0.257   -0.363    0.000
ATOM     2  H           1      0.257    0.727    0.000
ATOM     3  H           1      0.771   -0.727    0.890
ATOM     4  H           1      0.771   -0.727   -0.890
TER      5              1
END
```

The first line is the molecule's common name. The second gives the file's author and the date the file was created. Each of the *ATOM* lines then specifies the type and location of a single atom. It's not obvious what the *TER* line is for or why there's a *1* in the fourth column of each *ATOM* line, but we probably don't care.

It's tempting to start writing code immediately, but experience[2] teaches that it's worth taking a moment to check our assumptions about the input format. For example, can PDB files have blank lines? And do the *CMPND* and *AUTHOR* lines always appear first and in that order?

As I tell my undergrad students, "An hour of hard work can often save you sixty seconds on Google." A search for *PDB format* turns up dozens of links, including a formal specification[3] written in the kind of pseudo-lawyerese that programmers slip into when they think someone in a suit and tie might be listening. Hmm...it looks like PDB files can contain dozens of different types of records, organized in several different sections. All we want are atoms' coordinates, so for now, we'll just skip over anything we don't recognize and see what happens.

---

[2] "Experience is simply the name we give our mistakes." —Oscar Wilde
[3] http://www.rcsb.org/pdb/docs/format/pdbguide2.2/guide2.2_frame.html

---

\\// **Joe Asks...**
ɔ̣ʃ
ᴕ   <u>**Can You Do That?**</u>

Ignoring things we don't recognize sounds like a recipe for trouble. What if there are atoms on lines that don't start with the word *ATOM*? What if some non-*ATOM* lines modify the meaning of *ATOM* lines? Shouldn't we read the spec, highlighter in hand, and *then* write our program?

In this case, the answer is "no." Reading the PDB spec would take longer than translating all of the molecule files by hand. Doing so *might* prevent a few mistakes, but the cost of those mistakes is pretty much zero. It would be irresponsible of us to take this lackadaisacal attitude toward hospital patient records, or settings for the engines on commercial passenger jets, but the pragmatic approach here is to do what's simplest and fix it later if we need to. It's crucial, though, to understand what the output is supposed to be so that we can spot errors if and when we make them.

Now, let's take another look at our output format:

```
-- Nitrogen
1 17 0.5 0.257 -0.363 0.000
-- Hydrogens
1 6 0.2 0.257 0.727 0.000
1 6 0.2 0.771 -0.727 0.890
1 6 0.2 0.771 -0.727 -0.890
```

The lines beginning with a double dash are obviously comments; it's safe to assume we can generate whatever we want for them, or nothing at all. The other columns are *1*, meaning "this is a sphere"; a color code; the atom's radius; and its XYZ coordinates.

Right away, it's obvious that we'll want some sort of lookup table to translate from PDB's *N*s and *H*s to the first three columns of the VU3 file. Let's set that problem aside for the moment, though, and concentrate on getting the XYZ coordinates out of the PDB file. The general outline of our program is

```
for each PDB file:
    read atoms from file
    figure out what to call the output file
    write atoms and other data to that file
```

In Python, this is

```
import sys

for inputName in sys.argv[1:]:
    atoms = readPdb(inputName)
    outputName = translateName(inputName)
    writeVu3(outputName, atoms)
```

Extracting atoms from the PDB file is pretty simple: all we have to do is select those lines that begin with the word *ATOM* and split them into fields. The third field tells us what kind of atom it is, while the fifth, sixth, and seventh give us its XYZ coordinates. Python lists are indexed from zero (just like arrays in C and Java), so we actually use 2 and 4 as our starting indices, rather than 3 and 5:

```
def readPdb(inputName):
    input = open(inputName, 'r')
    result = []
    for line in input:
        if line[:4] == 'ATOM':
            fields = line.split()
            atom = fields[2] + fields[4:7]
            result.append(atom)
    input.close()
    return result
```

line.split() breaks a string into pieces. It can use anything as a divider—the expression line.split(';'), for example, would split it on semicolons—but the default is to split on whitespace, which is exactly what we want here.

Notice that we're not bothering to check for format errors in the input. If an *ATOM* line has fewer fields than expected, for example, then *fields[2] + fields[4:7]* could throw an out-of-bounds exception. Big deal—if it happens, the program will print out a stack trace and halt. That wouldn't be good enough for a shrink-wrapped product, but it's fine for a little data crunching utility.

Before going any further, let's check that this simple function does what it's supposed to do. Running the code in a debugger, and checking the *atoms* list returned by readPdb(), is one way. Another is to modify the main loop to print the list of atoms to the screen:

```
for inputName in sys.argv[1:]:
    atoms = readPdb(inputName)
    for a in atoms:
        print a
    outputName = translateName(inputName)
    writeVu3(outputName, atoms)
```

Let's run this on ammonia.pdb:

```
Traceback (most recent call last):
  File "pdb2vu3.py", line 15, in ?
    atoms = readPdb(inputName)
  File "pdb2vu3.py", line 7, in readPdb
    atom = fields[2] + fields[4:7]
TypeError: cannot concatenate 'str' and 'list' objects
```

Whoops: *fields[2]* selects a single string from the list, but *fields[4:7]* creates a new sublist, and Python doesn't know which way we want it to concatenate the string and the list. Every language has cases like this, where ideas that make sense on their own bump into each other. One of the reasons Python, Ruby, and Java are gaining ground on languages like Perl and C++ is that the former are built on a

small number of strong principles, which makes such collisions rarer. The fix is
simply to turn the string into a list by wrapping it in []:

```
def readPdb(inputName):
    input = open(inputName, 'r')
    result = []
    for line in input:
        if line[:4] == 'ATOM':
            fields = line.split()
            atom = [fields[2]] + fields[4:7]
            result.append(atom)
    input.close()
    return result
```

The output is now

```
['N', '0.257', '-0.363', '0.000']
['H', '0.257', '0.727', '0.000']
['H', '0.771', '-0.727', '0.890']
['H', '0.771', '-0.727', '-0.890']
```

The point of this example isn't this little bug; the point is that I tested that my
input function was working before going on to the next step. One of the main
reasons to separate input, processing, and output in data crunching programs is
that doing so makes incremental testing possible.

The next step is to figure out what each output file should be called. The rule is
pretty simple: replace the .pdb on the end of the input file's name with .vu3:

```
def translateName(inputName):
    return inputName[:-4] + '.vu3'
```

Before the Python puritan in the back row starts screaming, yes, the "right" way
to peel the extension off a filename is to use os.path.splitext(). Since I'm writing this
code for my own use, expect to run it only a few times, can rerun it if anything
goes wrong, and don't want to confuse people by pulling in a pile of libraries they
haven't seen before, I'll cut this particular corner.

It's finally time to write the VU3 file—or is it? We still haven't decided how to
translate the PDB's atomic symbols into the shape code, color, and radius that
VU3 requires. The simplest way is probably just to hard-code a lookup table
into the program; if we make the program fail with an error message whenever it
runs into a type of atom it doesn't know how to translate, we can build this table
incrementally based on our input. This gives us

```
Lookup = {
    'H' : (1,  6, 0.2),
    'N' : (1, 17, 0.5)
}
def writeVu3(outputName, atoms):
    output = open(outputName, 'w')
    for (symbol, X, Y, Z) in atoms:
        if symbol not in Lookup:
```

```
        print >> sys.stderr, 'Unknown atom "%s"' % symbol
        sys.exit(1)
    shape, color, radius = Lookup[symbol]
    print >> output, shape, color, radius, X, Y, Z
output.close()
```

Lookup tables like this are almost always easier to read, and easier to maintain, than *if/then/else* branches in code. In fact, one of the things that makes agile languages like Python so usable is that it's so much easier to say what you want in a data structure than it is in a sturdy language like Java.

All right, we can now translate one PDB file into one VU3 file. Can we translate a second? Let's jump in at the deep end and try menthol, which has thirty-one atoms. Almost immediately, our program prints

```
Unknown atom "C"
```

Good—it's supposed to do that. After editing the program to add entries to the lookup table for carbon and oxygen (which also appears in menthol), our program produces the VU3 file we want.

Time to try it out for real. After copying all 112 PDB files into a temporary directory, I run

```
$ python pdb2vu3.py *.pdb
```

It takes four runs to turn up all of the unknown atoms (sulfur, chlorine, iron, and bromine). It also turns out that some atoms' symbols are spelled both in upper case, like *CL*, and mixed case, like *Cl*. Inconsistencies like this crop up all the time in data crunching; while it may be obvious to human beings that all of these strings mean the same thing, we still have to teach our programs to handle them properly.

We have two choices: add duplicate entries to the lookup table for each atom, or normalize the atoms' symbols. The first gives us a lookup table that looks like this:

```
Lookup = {
    'BR' : (1,  2, 0.9),
    'Br' : (1,  2, 0.9),
    'C'  : (1,  3, 0.5),
    'CL' : (1,  8, 0.6),
    'Cl' : (1,  8, 0.6),
    'FE' : (1, 13, 1.1),
    'Fe' : (1, 13, 1.1),
    'H'  : (1,  6, 0.2),
    'N'  : (1, 17, 0.5),
    'O'  : (1, 19, 0.5),
    'S'  : (1, 17, 0.7)
}
```

DRY
___

The general principle here is *DRY*: Don't Repeat Yourself (HT00). If you duplicate information in two or more places, sooner or later, you'll forget to update one of the copies and then lose hours tracking down the bug, muttering "But I *know* I fixed that!" the whole time. As always, you shouldn't use the fact that your data crunching program is going to be run only a few times as an excuse for sloppy practices; experience shows that throwaway code often isn't and that bad habits have a way of carrying over into everything you do.

This is a reasonable choice under the circumstances: the number of duplicated lines is small, they can be created by copying and pasting other lines, and if we ever forget one, our program will complain.

But what if atom names appeared in *every* combination of upper and lower case? What if, for example, iron appeared as *FE*, *Fe*, *fE*, and *fe*? Instead of doubling just the two-letter entries, we'd have to double all the single-letter ones, and then have four lines for those atoms with two-letter symbols.

It seems pretty unlikely that someone would write *fE* for iron, but if we were processing Canadian postal codes, every hundredth record or so would be *M5v 2p4* instead of *M5V 2P4*, or some other variation on the officially approved form.[4] In general, the more data you have to process, the more likely it is that at least some of it will be badly formatted.

And what happens if we decide to change the color or radius of the spheres representing iron atoms? If we have four entries for iron in our table, we'll have to remember to change all four. Again, it wouldn't particularly matter in this case if we missed one, but if we were processing thousands of files containing several dozen types of atoms, the odds are pretty good that sooner or later we'd wind up drawing balls of different colors or sizes for the same kind of atom.

This brings us to the second option: normalizing the atoms' symbols. If we decide that these will always be translated into title case (i.e., *Fe* and *Cl*), no matter what actually appeared in the input file, then our lookup table needs only one entry per atom. If we do this, though, we should include a comment to remind ourselves later that what we're manipulating isn't exactly what we read in. It'll take an extra

---

[4]Human beings are only partly to blame for this. If your word processor doesn't recognize Canadian postal codes, its capitalization "correcter" can easily turn *M5V* into *M5v*.

ten seconds to type in, but it might save us a couple of false starts if and when we spot an error in the output and have to fix a bug.

And we still have a choice to make. Should the symbols for atoms be normalized as the PDB file is being read? Or should we make a separate pass over the list of atoms and modify their symbols in place? In order to keep each function short (and testable), let's do the second. Our main loop becomes

```
for inputName in sys.argv[1:]:
    atoms = readPdb(inputName)
    normalizeSymbols(atoms)
    outputName = translateName(inputName)
    writeVu3(outputName, atoms)
```

and the new function normalizeSymbols() is

```
def normalizeSymbols(atoms):
    for record in atoms:
        record[0] = record[0].capitalize()
```

Remember, each element of *atoms* is a list whose elements are substrings from the line that was read in. If the line is properly formatted, its zeroth element is the atom's name. The capitalize() puts strings in title case, i.e., converts *aBC* to *Abc*.

Now, time for a confession. When I first wrote this code, I never actually considered duplicating lines in the lookup table. After tackling dozens of variations on this problem over the years, normalization has become a habit, as has handling each aspect of the translation in a separate transformation. These habits may not produce the optimal solution every time, but they always produce a good one, and they save me from having to think each case through.

2.3 Handling Multiline Records

Now that we know how to process files line by line, it's time to try reading ones in which records can take up several lines. To make things concrete, we'll build a parser to read the .ini configuration files used to store settings on older versions of Microsoft Windows and translate their contents into XML. I had to do this several years ago, when a company I was consulting for upgraded to a new version of a CAD program and wanted to bring everyone's old preferences over to the new system.

Like many legacy files, Windows configuration files use their own idiosyncratic syntax that has grown increasingly more complex over time. We don't need to address all of those peculiar quirks and oddities here; for our purposes, let's just go with the following list.

- A .ini file contains zero or more *sections*.
- Each section has a *title* and a *body*; the body may be empty.
- A title consists of a line containing just text inside square brackets, such as *[laser6]* or *[recently used]*. No section title may appear more than once in any file.
- The body contains zero or more properties. Each property consists of a key and a value separated by an =, as in *color=blue* or *file3=C:\book\intro.pml*.
- Comments begin with # and extend to the end of the line.

A typical file looks like this:

```
# Installation settings
[Bootstrap]
Location=$SYSUSERCONFIG/sversion.ini
BaseInstallation=$ORIGIN/..
buildid=645m44(Build:8784)
InstallMode=STANDALONE&ALL_USERS
ProductPatch=                              # empty

# Error handling
[ErrorReport]
ErrorReportPort=80
ErrorReportServer=services.caribou.org
```

For the moment, we'll ignore the special meaning of the values beginning with $ and concentrate on reading the file so that we can print it out like this:

```
<configure>
<section title="Bootstrap">
  <entry key="Location">$SYSUSERCONFIG/sversion.ini</entry>
  <entry key="BaseInstallation">$ORIGIN/..</entry>
  <entry key="buildid">645m44(Build:8784)</entry>
  <entry key="InstallMode">STANDALONE&amp;ALL_USERS</entry>
  <entry key="ProductPatch"></entry>
</section>
<section title="ErrorReport">
  <entry key="ErrorReportPort">80</entry>
  <entry key="ErrorReportServer">services.caribou.org</entry>
</section>
</configure>
```

Reading this file is going to be trickier than reading PDB files since we have to worry about which section each line is in. The simplest approach is probably to filter out the stuff we don't care about as we're reading the input file, process whatever is left, and then write the result as XML. Oh, and we'd better translate characters like &, <, and > into the *&*, *<*, and *>* that XML requires.

Let's start with our usual skeleton:

```
for inputName in sys.argv[1:]:
    lines = readIni(inputName)
    settings = process(lines)
    outputName = translateName(inputName)
    writeXml(outputName, settings)
```

The readIni() method doesn't just read lines from a file; it has to strip out comments and blank lines as well. The simplest way to do this is to delete the comment if one is present and then strip leading and trailing whitespace from what's left. If the result is the empty string, we throw it away.

If not, we append it to the list of lines being returned to the caller:

```
def readIni(inputName):
    input = open(inputName, 'r')
    result = []
    for line in input:

        # Get rid of everything from the first '#' (if there is one).
        first = line.find('#')
        if first >= 0:
            line = line[:first]

        # Strip leading and trailing whitespace.
        line = line.strip()

        # If nothing left, or what's left starts with '#', ignore the line.
        if not line:
            continue

        # Otherwise, save it.
        result.append(line)

    # Finish
    input.close()
    return result
```

That's pretty simple. It's also wrong—or at least, it *could* be wrong, if the # character is allowed to appear inside values. For example, is the following legal in an .ini file or not?

```
SongTitle="Love Potion #9" # last song played
```

If it is, then stripping everything after the first # will produce the wrong answer. What's worse, it will do so silently—instead of throwing an exception, it will throw data away.

We could solve this problem by searching each line for quotes and other markers. Regular expressions (which we'll meet in Chapter 3, *Regular Expressions*, on page 41) will make this much easier, so for now, we'll move on to the next step: translating the cleaned-up list of lines into XML.

To recap, the XML file we're writing has to start and end with *<configure>* and *</configure>*. Each time we see a section title, like *[this]*, we have to output *<section title="whatever">*. Oh, but we have to output *</section>* first to close the previous section. Also, every entry of the form *name=value* has to be written as <entry key="name">value</entry>.

No problem—the code is as follows.

```
def process(lines):
    result = ['<configure>']
    for line in lines:
        # Start of new section
        if line[0] == '[':
            # Close previous section
            result.append('</section>')

            # Start new section
            title = line[1:-1]
            result.append('<section title="%s">' % title)

        # Entry in current section
        else:
            key, value = line.split('=', 1)
            value = escape(value)
            result.append('   <entry key="%s">%s</entry>' % \
                          (key, value))

    # Done
    result.append('</configure>')
    return result
```

(The call line.split('=', 1) splits *line* on the first equals sign, returning at most two substrings.) The escape() function simply replaces characters that mean something special to XML with their equivalent escape sequences:

```
def escape(s):
    return s.replace('&', '&amp;')\
            .replace('<', '&lt;')\
            .replace('>', '&gt;')\
            .replace("'", '&apos;')\
            .replace('"', '&quot;')
```

So, is this program correct? Nope. Take a moment, and see if you can spot both of the errors. Or better yet, create a small .ini file, like this:

```
# Installation settings
[Bootstrap]
ProductKey=Caribou CAD 1.1
Location=$SYSUSERCONFIG/sversion.ini

# Error handling
[ErrorReport]
ErrorReportPort=80
```

and print out the list returned by process(). You should get

```
<configure>
</section>
<section title="Bootstrap">
  <entry key="ProductKey">Caribou CAD 1.1</entry>
  <entry key="Location">$SYSUSERCONFIG/sversion.ini</entry>
</section>
<section title="ErrorReport">
  <entry key="ErrorReportPort">80</entry>
</configure>
```

Two things are wrong. First, a closing </section> tag appears before the first opening tag <section title="Bootstrap"> because we always print a closing tag before an opening one, even for the first section. Second, we're *not* printing a closing </section> tag at the end of the last section—at the end of the input list, we close off the whole thing, without also closing the section we were reading.

The first bug is fixed by introducing a Boolean flag to keep track of whether the section we're about to open is the first section. The easy solution for the second bug is to always print out a closing </section> tag before the closing </configure>. But what happens if we have an empty .ini file as input? This "solution" would give us

```
<configure>
</section>
</configure>
```

We should print out the closing </section> tag only if we've seen at least one section. We could keep track of this with another Boolean flag. Alternatively, we can replace our previous Boolean with a counter. If the count is zero inside the loop, we don't output a closing </section> tag; if the count is nonzero outside the loop, we do. Our final function is

```
def process(lines):
    result = ['<configure>']
    count = 0
    for line in lines:
        # Start of new section
        if line[0] == '[':
            # Close previous section
            if count > 0:
                result.append('</section>')
            # Start new section
            title = line[1:-1]
            result.append('<section title="%s">' % title)
            count += 1
        # Entry in current section
        else:
            key, value = line.split('=', 1)
            value = escape(value)
            result.append('  <entry key="%s">%s</entry>' % \
                          (key, value))
    # Done
    if count > 0:
        result.append('</section>')
    result.append('</configure>')
    return result
```

Our program's last two functions are straightforward to write:

```
def translateName(inputName):
    return inputName[:-4] + '.xml'

def writeXml(outputName, settings):
    output = open(outputName, 'w')
    for line in settings:
        print >> output, line
    output.close()
```

Bracketing and Finite State Machines

Bracketing blocks of output with begin and end markers is a very common task. The general pattern for doing this if you're processing data one record at a time is

```
for (each input record)
    if (record is start-of-section marker)
        if (not first section)
            close previous section
        start new section
    else
        create output record
if (any sections created)
    close final section
```

Alternatively, if you're reading everything into memory anyway, you can do this:

```
for (each section)
    start new section
    for (each input record in section)
        create output record
    end section
```

The second approach makes the output logic easier to read and debug but requires you to create a more complicated data structure (basically, a list of lists, instead of a single flat list). This trade-off between the complexity of code and the complexity of data is a recurring theme when you're crunching data.

Good programmers use a formalism called *finite state machines* when designing parsers like these. State machines are outside the scope of this book, but (HF04) includes a very readable introduction.

A few simple tests were enough to convince me that these functions did what I wanted and that the program as a whole was done.

As the bugs in the process() function showed, the most likely place for bugs to creep in to data crunching programs is at the beginning and end of processing. When testing, you should therefore always try

- empty input (if the format allows it),

- a single record,

- two records (so that there's no "middle" record), and

- three or more records.

If the features you want to test are simple, you can create test data by copying and editing actual data files. If you're trying to test something obscure, it's often less work just to create a couple of input files yourself.

2.4 Checking for Collisions

Feeling pleased with myself, I mailed my program to my boss. Ten minutes later, my mailer bleeped. "It doesn't work. Come see me."

It took less than a minute to figure out what was wrong. The old CAD program allowed .ini files to reset values several times, as in the following example:

```
[View]
WindowSize=1024,768
BackgroundColor=green7
WindowSize=1280,1024
```

The new CAD program, on the other hand, allowed each value to be set only once per section. If an XML configuration file had multiple values for a single key, the CAD program crashed on start-up.

A quick peek inside a couple of real new-style configuration files convinced me that keys didn't actually have to be unique within sections. For example, the following seemed legal:

```
[View]
WindowSize=1024,768
BackgroundColor=green7
WindowSize=1280,1024

[Print]
BackgroundColor=green5
```

Hmm...this looks like a job for our friend Mr. Dictionary.

Dictionaries

More often than not, when data has to be unique, the solution to the problem involves using a dictionary. Depending on what language you're working with, dictionaries might be called *maps* (Java), *hashes* (Perl), or *associative arrays* (pretentious). In each case, they act like a two-column table, mapping keys (the things in the left column) to values (the things on the right). A price sheet is a good example of a dictionary; it maps items to their prices:

```
ANW-400    179.95
ANW-407    179.95
ANW-460    209.95
...
```

The key features of dictionaries are

- Any key can appear only once. A single dictionary can't, for example, have three entries for the ANW-400 left-handed U-bend clodwrangler. If you need to associate several pieces of data with a key, the usual trick is to store a list (or set) as the key's value.
- Keys aren't stored in any particular order. While the table above shows the keys in alphabetical order, the actual order could be reversed, or seem completely arbitrary. Any good textbook on data structures (such as [Sed97]) will explain why; all that's important right now is that this is a necessary side effect of the third feature.
- Lookup is fast. This is the whole point of using a dictionary rather than (for example) a list of pairs. Instead of checking each key (which takes N steps when there are N of them), a dictionary can find a key in a near-constant number of steps.[5] The difference doesn't matter when you have a few dozen items but can make or break your program when there's a million.

One final advantage of using dictionaries is that keys can be strings, objects, or whatever else you want—they don't have to be integers, like the indices of a list. In practice, most dictionaries have strings as keys, but you can use integers, XY coordinates, function pointers, or just about anything else.

So, suppose you have a list full of email addresses, and you want to count how many times each one appears. For example, the list might contain one entry for each time posting to a mailing list, and you'd like to see who the most frequent contributors are. An example of such a list is

```
see@spot.run.com
see@spot.run.com
jane@up-the-hill.org
see@spot.run.com
jane@up-the-hill.org
purple.dinosaur@bad.tv
jane@up-the-hill.org
```

This simple program will do the trick:

```
Line 1    import sys

          count = {}
          for address in sys.stdin:
5             address = address.rstrip()
              if address not in count:
                  count[address] = 1
              else:
                  count[address] += 1
10
          addresses = count.keys()
          addresses.sort()
          for address in addresses:
              print address, count[address]
```

---

[5]The actual time depends on how distinct your keys are, which in turn governs the likelihood of collisions; [Sed97] can give you the details.

Let's take a closer look at that program. Line 3 creates an empty dictionary and assigns it to *count*. The loop beginning at line 4 reads one email address at a time; line 5 strips trailing whitespace off it (e.g., the carriage return and/or newline, depending on whether you're on Unix or Windows). Line 6 then checks whether we've seen this address before. If we haven't, we add it to the dictionary with a count of 1. If we have, we add 1 to the value already associated with it.

The second part of this program then gets a list of the dictionary's keys, which are all the addresses we've seen (line 11), sorts it into alphabetical order (line 12), and then prints each address and the count associated with it. When run as:

```
python freq.py < email.txt
```

the program's output is

```
jane@up-the-hill.org 3
purple.dinosaur@bad.tv 1
see@spot.run.com 3
```

For the record, we can accomplish the same thing almost as easily in Java (note that we have to use *Integer* objects to count addresses, instead of primitive integers, because only objects can be put into Java dictionaries).

```java
import java.util.*;
import java.io.*;
class Freq {
    public static void main(String[] args) {
        BufferedReader input =
            new BufferedReader(new InputStreamReader(System.in));
        Map m = new HashMap();
        String line;
        try {
            while ((line = input.readLine()) != null) {
                line = line.trim();
                if (m.containsKey(line)) {
                    Integer tmp = (Integer)m.get(line);
                    m.put(line, new Integer(tmp.intValue() + 1));
                } else {
                    m.put(line, new Integer(1));
                }
            }
            input.close();
        }
        catch (IOException e) {
            System.err.println(e);
        }
        Set keySet = m.keySet();
        List keyList = new LinkedList(keySet);
        Collections.sort(keyList);
        for (Iterator i=keyList.iterator(); i.hasNext(); ) {
            String key = (String)i.next();
            Integer value = (Integer)m.get(key);
            System.out.println(key + " " + value);
        }
    }
}
```

All right, it's two-and-a-half times longer than the equivalent Python program, it isn't as fast on small files,[6] and we have to compile it before we can run it, but other than *that*, it's almost as easy....

Configuration Files Revisited

So, back to making sure that our XML configuration files try to set any particular value only once in a given section. The function that reads the .ini file doesn't need any changes; the function that escapes special characters like &, <, and > doesn't either, but process() must be changed.

Let's create an empty dictionary each time a new section starts. As we process keys and values, we add them to that dictionary. If a key appears two (or more) times, the later value simply overwrites the earlier one so that final value is the last one seen:

```python
def process(lines):
    result = []
    section = None
    content = {}
    for line in lines:

        # Start of new section
        if line[0] == '[':
            # Save old values (if any)
            if section:
                entry = [section, content]
                result.append(entry)

            # Start a new section
            section = line[1:-1]
            content = {}

        # Add to the current dictionary.
        else:
            key, value = line.split("=", 1)
            content[key] = escape(value)

    # Finish
    if section:
        entry = [section, content]
        result.append(entry)
    return result
```

Once again, this function has to watch out for the special cases at the start and end of input. Other than that, it's straightforward. The result it hands back to the caller is a list of pairs. The first element of each pair is the section title, while the second element is the dictionary holding the final value associated with each key in that section.

---

[6]Java runs faster than Python because Java checks the types of variables once during compilation, instead of having to check them repeatedly at runtime like Python. However, Java's virtual machine is a lot larger than Python's, and its libraries are larger still. For small input files, the time required to load the JVM into memory overshadows the fact that it's faster once it's running.

Since we've changed the format of the data structure that process() creates, we have to change writeXml() as well:

```python
def writeXml(outputName, settings):
    output = open(outputName, 'w')
    print >> output, '<configure>'
    for (section, content) in settings:
        print >> output, '<%s>' % section
        for key in content:
            value = content[key]
            print >> output, '  <%s>%s</%s>' % (key, value, key)
        print >> output, '</%s>' % section
    print >> output, '</configure>'
    output.close()
```

Finally, we have to test. It's always important to, but it's especially important when the first "solution" didn't do what the boss expected. Here's a made-up .ini file that covers the important bases:

```
[Section1]
Key=a
Key=b

[Section2]
Key=c

[Section3]
Red=crimson
Green=lime
Red=vermilion
Green=chartreuse

[Section4]
```

And here's the output:

```
<configure>
<Section1>
  <Key>b</Key>
</Section1>
<Section2>
  <Key>c</Key>
</Section2>
<Section3>
  <Green>chartreuse</Green>
  <Red>vermilion</Red>
</Section3>
<Section4>
</Section4>
</configure>
```

Um, hang on. Take a look at *Section3*. In the .ini file, *Red* appears before *Green*. In the .xml file, on the other hand, it appears after. Is this a bug?

Nope. It's a feature. As we said earlier, dictionaries store keys in arbitrary order. In this case, the dictionary has decided that it wants *Green* before *Red*, even though that's the reverse of what was in the input stream.

Is this a problem? That depends on whether the order of keys in a section matters, which in turn depends on the CAD package that's reading them. If the CAD package doesn't care, we don't have to either. If it does, we can modify our code—for example, so that the dictionary stores a list of settings for each key, in the order they were seen.

2.5 Including One File in Another

Luckily, the order of keys didn't matter. Something else did come up, though. In the process of converting everyone's old .ini configuration files to XML, I discovered that .ini files could refer to one another so that common settings could be stored in one place. For example, one of the company's engineering groups had .ini files that looked like this:

```
%general.ini%

[View]
WindowSize=1024,768
BackgroundColor=green7
WindowSize=1280,1024
```

where general.ini was

```
[Drawing]
LineWidth=2
Corners=Rounded

[File]
DefaultName=$PROJECT.$VERSION
DefaultTitle=off
```

Unfortunately, the new XML configuration files didn't support this feature: every one of the new files had to stand on its own.

All right, how many files were we talking about? Roughly eighty engineers in the company used this CAD package; of those, only fifteen had configuration files that included other ones, and none of those inclusions was recursive (i.e., no-one had a file that included a second, which in turn included a third). Since the configuration files had to be converted only once, I decided that the simplest thing to do was to copy those fifteen configuration files, insert the included data using a text editor, then recrunch just those files.

This took about twenty minutes, most of which was spent tracking down a sys admin to get permission to read all the engineers' accounts. If there had been 100 files to process, though, or if I'd had to process files repeatedly, I would have upgraded ini2xml.py.

As always, I would have started by figuring out where to make the change. One way is to write another filter function, which replaces any inclusions in the list of lines produced by readIni() with the contents of the included file. That would work fine if inclusions only ever went one level deep, but if recursive inclusion was allowed, I'd need some kind of loop, like this:

```
lines = readIni(filename)
while containsIncludes(lines):
    index = findFirstInclude(lines)
    expansion = readIni(index)
    lines = insert(lines, index, expansion)
```

That doesn't look too bad—but if you've had to expand included files in other data crunching problems, alarm bells should already be ringing in your head. What would this bit of code do when presented with a file like selfinclusion.ini, which includes itself?

```
[Foo]
a = b
%selfinclusion.ini%
```

The first loop will expand this to

```
[Foo]
a = b
[Foo]
a = b
%selfinclusion.ini%
```

The second will expand it to

```
[Foo]
a = b
[Foo]
a = b
[Foo]
a = b
%selfinclusion.ini%
```

and so on until memory runs out or the user hits Ctrl-C.

This seems like a pretty unlikely case. After all, who would include a file in itself? What actually does come up pretty often, though, is mutual recursion: file A includes B, which includes C, which includes A again (Figure 2.1 on page 31). This happens all the time in C and C++, in which many of the standard library's header files depend on one another.

The standard solution is to keep track of which files you are currently expanding and halt if you ever encounter one you're already in. We can implement this by making readIni() recurse as soon as it sees an inclusion. Along with the name of the file currently being read, readIni() must keep a list (technically, a stack) of the files it is currently processing. When it sees an inclusion line, it figures out which file is being included and then checks to make sure it isn't already expanding that file by checking whether the filename is already on the stack. If not, it pushes the file's name on the stack, calls itself to read that file, and then adds the result to the list of lines it's building up. The whole thing is shown in the following listing.

```
def error(msg):
    print >> sys.stderr, msg
    sys.exit(1)

def readIni(inputName, stack):
    input = open(inputName, 'r')
    result = []
    for line in input:
        # This part stays the same
        line = line.strip()
        first = line.find('#')
        if first >= 0:
            line = line[:first]
        if (not line) or (line[0] == '#'):
            continue

        # Regular line
        if line[0] != '%':
            result.append(line)

        # Inclusion
        else:
            filename = line[1:-1]
            if filename in stack:
                error("Recursive inclusion of %s: %s" % \
                        (filename, repr(stack)))
            newStack = stack + [filename]
            inclusion = readIni(filename, newStack)
            result = result + inclusion
    return result
```

and the call in the main body of the program is

```
lines = readIni(inputName, [inputName])
```

Time to test it. Does it do the right thing on files that don't include other files? Yes. Does it do the right thing on selfinclusion.ini? Yes, it halts with an error message almost instantly.[7] All right, what about the "A includes B includes C includes A" case? It only takes few seconds to create three files and run the program. Bingo! It does the right thing.

Lessons Learned

This little exercise highlights two important points about data crunching. The first is that the job isn't done until it's done: your first solution to a data crunching problem will often miss a few corner cases, so it's important to write readable code, even if you're planning to throw it away once the job is done. It's just as important to store that code in whatever version control system you use for your "real" programs so that you (and your colleagues) can find it days or weeks later.

---

[7]If we were in a more forgiving mood, the program could just stop recursing when it encountered a file it was already in the midst of including.

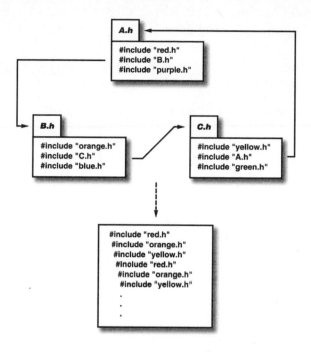

Figure 2.1: CYCLIC INCLUSION

The second point is how important it is to master a programmable editor, such as Emacs or Vim. I didn't edit the fifteen files that used inclusion one by one; instead, I recorded a macro while editing the first one and then ran it fourteen more times. (I also saved it, just in case.) I wouldn't do this if I needed nested loops or data structures,[8] but a surprising number of simple data crunching problems don't.

2.6 The Unix Shell

If success is measured by longevity, then the Unix shell[9] is the most successful data crunching environment in history. Now almost thirty-five years old, it is still many programmers' favorite way to move information around.

---

[8]However, someone who had mastered Emacs Lisp might.

[9]Strictly speaking, there's no such thing as "the" shell—there are actually dozens, including the venerable /bin/sh, and my personal favorite, bash. In this book, I will stick to tools and syntax that will work with (almost) all of them.

As its creators have observed [KP99], the shell owes its power to its "lots of little tools" philosophy. Instead of offering programmers a small number of all-singing, all-dancing tools, it gives them dozens of smaller ones, each of which does one job well. What's more, the shell makes it easy to combine those tools in lots of different ways and to add new tools to the mix.

The key to making this work is that every well-behaved Unix tool follows three simple conventions:

- Read from standard input, and write to standard output, unless you're told to do otherwise.
- Expect lines of text as input, and produce lines of text as output.
- If all goes well, return a status code of 0 to the shell. Any other value will be interpreted as signaling an error.

redirection

pipes

That's it—those are the only rules a program has to obey in order to play well with hundreds of others. The reason is that if a program obeys these rules, then programmers can combine it with others using *redirection* and *pipes*. Redirection means reading from a file instead of from standard input or writing to a file instead of to standard output. The former is done using the < character, like this:

```
myprog < somefile.txt     # get input from somefile.txt
```

while the latter uses '>', like this:

```
myprog > anotherfile.txt  # send output to anotherfile.txt
```

For example, suppose you want to save the names of all the Java files in some directory to a file. The program that creates the listing is called ls, but it usually sends its output to the screen. No problem; all you have to do is this:

```
ls *.java > javafiles.txt
```

A pipe simply connects the output of one program to the input of another. For example, suppose you want to find out how many Python files there are in a directory. ls will list them for you, and wc will count the number of characters, words, and lines in its input:

```
ls *.py | wc
```

If I do this in the directory where I've put examples for this chapter, the output is

```
10     10     147
```

Ten lines, ten words (there's one filename per line), and 147 characters in total. If we wanted to save this result to a file, we could combine redirection and piping:

```
ls *.py | wc > numfiles.txt
```

and so on. It's as flexible and as powerful as a programming language.

In fact, the shell *is* a programming language, complete with loops, conditionals, variables, and functions. Here's a little program that uses it to find the home directory of each user whose login ID appears in a file:

```
cat $1 | while read uid
do
    echo $uid
    grep $uid /etc/passwd | cut -d : -f 5
done
```

Given an input file like this:

```
gvwilson:x:182:9:Greg Wilson:/h/6/gvwilson:/bin/bash
dave:x:180:7:Dave Thomas:/h/3/dave:/bin/bash
andy:x:181:7:Andy Hunt:/h/3/andy:/bin/tcsh
alant:x:196:9:Alan Turing:/h/6/alant:/bin/tcsh
```

we'd run this program like this:

```
./findhome.sh findhome-in.txt
```

and get this output

```
gvwilson
/h/6/gvwilson
dave
/h/3/dave
andy
/h/3/andy
alant
/h/6/alant
```

Let's break it down:

- *$1* is the first command-line argument (the script's name is the zeroth), so *cat $1* prints the contents of the file to standard output.

- ...Except that instead of going to the stream, this script pipes the output of cat to a *while* loop, which puts one line at a time in a variable called *uid*.

- The body of the loop uses echo to print the user ID to the screen. Note the $ in front of the variable name; this is how you tell the shell that you want to replace the variable's name with its value.

- The next line uses grep to find the user ID in /etc/passwd, which is the central password file on most Unix systems. Any lines that match will be sent through a pipe to the cut command. This is actually a little bit sloppy: if the input file contains *fred*, for example, grep will match *fred*, *freddie*, *alfred*, and anything else with those four letters in the right order. We'll see in the next chapter how to make grep be a little more selective.

- Finally, cut breaks its input into fields by splitting it on colons (the *-d* flag) and then selects the fifth one (the *-f*), which is where the user's home directory is stored.

cat	Concatenate and display text files.
cd	Change working directory.
chmod	Change file and directory permissions.
cut	Select fields from data.
cp	Copy files and directories.
date	Display the current date and time.
diff	Show differences between two text files.
du	Print the disk space used by files and directories.
echo	Print arguments.
env	Show environment variables.
find	Find files or directories with specific properties.
grep	Print lines matching a pattern.
head	Display the first few lines of a file.
lpr	Send a file to a printer.
ls	List files and directories.
man	Documentation for commands.
mkdir	Make directories.
mv	Move (rename) files and directories.
od	Dump file contents in a variety of formats.
ps	Display status of running processes.
pwd	Print current working directory.
rm	Remove files.
rmdir	Remove directories.
sort	Sort lines.
tail	Display the last few lines of a file.
tar	Archive files.
uniq	Remove duplicate lines.
wc	Count lines, words, and characters in a file.
zip	Package and compress files.

Figure 2.2: USEFUL COMMANDS

It takes a little getting used to, but once you know how to drive the shell, you can accomplish a lot with just a few keystrokes. Figure 2.2 lists some commands that are particularly useful for crunching data, along with a brief description of what each does.

The command line provides an easy way to do simple things and has a better keystroke-to-result ratio than almost anything else, but you should always keep its limitations in mind. The most important of these, from a data crunching point of view, is its lack of data structures.[10] As far as the classic Unix model is concerned, everything is a list of strings. If you need something more sophisticated, like a tree, you'll probably find it easier to use Python, Ruby, or one of their kin. Alternatively, you can invest in a commercial tool such as Crystal Software's TextPipe Pro (http://www.crystalsoftware.com.au/), which will let you apply the pipe model to a wide variety of nontext formats as well.

Creating a Well-Behaved Tool

I said earlier that well-behaved command-line tools should be able to read from standard input and write to standard output so that programmers can pipe them together. It's usually not worth going the extra mile to do this for a one-off data cruncher, but if there's any reasonable chance that your program is going to hang around, or if you're planning to solve your problem one piece at a time, there are a few conventions you should follow (even though some standard Unix tools don't):

- short (single-letter) command-line flags should start with a dash, as in -p;

- long (multiletter) command-line flags should start with a double dash, as in --print;

- if no filenames are specified, the program should read from standard input, and write to standard output;

- if a single filename is specified, the program should read from it and write to standard output;

- if two filenames are specified, the program should read from the first and write to the second;

- alternatively, if one or more filenames are specified, the program should read from each in turn and send all output to standard output;

- error messages should go to standard error (so that they'll appear on the screen even when the program's output is being piped to another tool); and

- if all goes well, your program should return a status code of 0, since the shell interprets a nonzero code as an error signal.

For example, suppose we want to sample a data set by taking every N^{th} line; if the user doesn't specify anything else with -n, the program will set N to 10. It will read from all the files the user specifies (standard input if none is listed), unless the -o argument is used, in which case it will write to that file.

The first step is to process the command-line arguments:

---

[10]However, Microsoft's next-generation shell, code-named Monad, may provide them.

```python
        # Set flags.
        input = []
        output = None
        sampling = None

        # Process command-line arguments.
        argdex = 1
        while argdex < len(sys.argv):
            if sys.argv[argdex] in ["-n", "--number"]:
                if sampling is not None:
                    fail("Sampling rate specified too many times")
                argdex, arg = getArg(argdex, sys.argv)
                try:
                    sampling = int(arg)
                except ValueError:
                    fail("Need integer for -n/--number, not '%s'" % arg)
                if sampling <= 0:
                    fail("Sampling rate must be positive (not %d)" % sampling)
            elif sys.argv[argdex] in ["-o", "--output"]:
                if output is not None:
                    fail("Too many output files specified")
                argdex, arg = getArg(argdex, sys.argv)
                try:
                    output = open(arg, "w")
                except IOError:
                    fail("Unable to open '%s' for output" % arg)
            elif sys.argv[argdex][0] == "-":
                fail("Unknown flag '%s'" % sys.argv[argdex])
            else:
                input.append(sys.argv[argdex])
            argdex += 1
    # Check arguments, filling in defaults.
    if input == []:
        input = ["-"]
    if output is None:
        output = sys.stdout
    if sampling is None:
        sampling = 10
```

Since we may need to record multiple input files, *input* is set to an empty list. If it's still an empty list after all the arguments have been processed, the user wants us to read from standard input. *output* and *sampling* are set to *None* so that we can tell whether the user has tried to set them multiple times. (If we assigned them their default values before processing arguments, we wouldn't be able to spot this.) And yes, there's a lot of error handling: if it's worth making this program reusable, it's worth helping people use it.

The helper functions argument processing relies on are simple:

```python
    # Print an error message and die.
    def fail(msg):
        print >> sys.stderr, msg
        sys.exit(1)

    # Get an argument, or fail.
    def getArg(argdex, args):
```

> ## Joe Asks...
>
> ### Do I Have to Write This Much Code Every Time?
>
> No. Most languages have libraries for processing command-line arguments, usually called something like getopt. I've written the argument processing out by hand in this example so that you can see how such a library might be implemented.

```
flag = args[argdex]
if argdex >= len(args)-1:
    fail("%s requires an argument" % flag)
return argdex+2, args[argdex+1]
```

The program's main body is also simple:

```
# Process a single input file/stream.
def process(filename, output, sampling):
    if filename == "-":
        stream = sys.stdin
    else:
        try:
            stream = open(filename, "r")
        except IOError:
            fail("Unable to open '%s' for input" % filename)
    count = 0
    for line in stream:
        count += 1
        if count == sampling:
            output.write(line)
            count = 0
    stream.close()

# Process data.
for filename in input:
    process(filename, output, sampling)
output.close()
```

The only clever bit is the check inside process() to see whether the input file's name is a dash. If it is, the program reads from standard input, rather than a file. This way, the user can control whether the program reads from other files and then standard input, or vice versa.

You may be able to simplify this even further, depending on what language you're using. In Python, for example, you can use the fileinput module; it automatically cycles through the files specified on the command line, so that this:

```
import sys, fileinput
for line in fileinput.input():
    doSomething(line)
```

processes each line from each input file, in order. It even knows that - means "standard input."

This is even simpler in Perl:

```
while (<>) {
    doSomething($_);
}
```

The diamond, <>, is the default file handle, while the odd-looking symbol $_ is Perl's way of saying, "whatever the programmer is most likely to care about right now."

2.7 Very Large Data Sets

Parkinson's Law [Par93] states that work expands to fill the time available. Programmers have repeatedly discovered that data behaves the same way: no matter how many disks you have, they're all 99% full, 99% of the time.

What this means for data crunching is that there are times when you can't fit all of your data into memory at once. A year's worth of web server access logs, for example, can be 10 or 15 gigabytes long; if your operating system only allows processes 1 or 2 gigabytes of virtual address space, you have to process it in chunks.

If you're lucky, you can do this by breaking your crunching into two steps. The first filters the raw data to create something small enough to be loaded into memory; the second then does whatever you originally wanted to do. For example, suppose your company handled a billion transactions last year, and you want to find the million largest. If you can store only 100 million records in memory at a time, you could do this:

```
for (each block of 100 million records)
    read into memory
    sort
    append the million largest to a temporary file
read the temporary file (which is 10 million records long)
sort
print the million largest records
```

out-of-core algorithms

But what if you can't handle the data in chunks? For example, what if you're processing multispectral satellite images, or a CAT scan of someone's head, and really do need all 22 gigabytes at once? In that case, you have to use *out-of-core algorithms*. Many of these date from the days of mainframes and tape drives; almost all are more complicated than their in-memory counterparts. If you find yourself in this territory, you're no longer "just" crunching data; it's time to step away from the keyboard and do some real analysis and design.

Data Structures 101

Lists and dictionaries are the workhorses of data crunching, but sometimes the right way to solve a problem is to dust off some of those CompSci 101 lecture notes in the bottom of your closet. For example, you can select the million largest records from a set of a billion using a *priority queue*, which is a list in which *q[k]* is always greater than *q[2*k+1]* and *q[2*k+2]*. Each time you add an item to the list, the queue reorders the existing items to maintain this rule. If you limit its size to a million, then feed it a billion records one by one, the end result will be the million largest records.

The standard Python library includes a priority queue module called heapq. Similar modules are available for most other languages; if yours doesn't have one, you can easily code one up from the description in (Sed97) or another data structures and algorithms textbook.

2.8 Summary

This chapter has introduced a lot of ideas and techniques. Some of them are specific to handling streams of text, but others come into play every time you crunch data. The most important are

- Start with something simple, and refine it as you discover cases it doesn't handle, rather than overengineering solutions to problems that don't exist. (In the Extreme Programming world, this goes by the name *YAGNI*: You Ain't Gonna Need It.)

- Separate input from processing, and processing from output: it makes each part easier to test, reuse, and evolve.

- Don't repeat yourself.

- Don't use the fact that your data crunching code isn't going out to a customer as an excuse to be sloppy. In the long run (and often, even in the short), modularizing your code, and testing as you go along, will get you the right answer sooner.

- Learn your tools. In particular, learn your way around your favorite language's standard library and the standard Unix tools, and master one programmable editor; all will pay rich dividends.

Chapter 3

Regular Expressions

Suppose you're building a web site for your partner's gardening business. Since you have some time on your hands,[1] you've decided to write the whole thing from scratch. You've created a form that will let people register with your site, and now you want to use the phone numbers they give you to find out where they are.

So you sit back and ask yourself, what exactly is a legal phone number? Ignore extensions for the moment, and assume that your customers live in North America.[2] A legal phone number is seven digits, optionally preceded by a three-digit area code. Simple, right?

Wrong. I usually type in phone numbers without any punctuation at all, like this: *416 555 1212*. My partner, on the other hand, prefers *416-555-1212*, while my brother likes *(416) 555-1212*. And then there's the whole question of leading zeroes and ones—if you're not careful about those, you can wind up dialing a pay-by-the-minute number in Tuvalu. Somehow, the web site has to extract two triples and a quad from all of these to feed to the library that translates phone numbers into postal codes.

The wrong way to solve this problem is to strip whitespace off the user's strings, split what's left into pieces, and then scan it a character at a time, skipping over punctuation, to count digits and check that no one's blunt fingers have entered *(416) 5t5-1w12* or *416-555-!212* by mistake. Handling just one format this way is tedious; handling all the ones people use on a daily basis would leave you with a steaming brown pile of loops and conditionals that would be a perpetual headache to maintain.

---

[1] More accurately, if you don't look busy, you'll have to help empty the compost.

[2] This is often a self-fulfilling assumption—if you don't accommodate Dutch, Australian, and Brazilian customers, you shouldn't be surprised if you don't get any—but that is a rant for another book....

The best solution is to use the power tools of text processing: *regular expressions* (REs). Most modern programming languages have an RE library; a few, like Perl and Ruby, have even made them part of the language itself. Using REs, programmers specify a pattern that they want a piece of text to match. These patterns can express very complex rules in a very compact way. When a match is found, the pattern remembers which bits of text lined up with which bits of the pattern so that the programmer can extract substrings of interest after the fact.

That's the good news; the bad news is that RE notation is one of the most cryptic programmers have ever created (and that says a lot). When mathematicians want to express a new idea, they can just squiggle some new symbols on a whiteboard. Programmers, on the other hand, are restricted to the punctuation on a standard keyboard. As a result, many symbols can have two or three meanings in an RE, depending on context. What's worse, different languages use slightly different syntaxes for regular expressions (Section 3.6, *Other Systems*, on page 71). You may have to read someone else's RE very carefully to understand what it does.

The Bible for regular expressions is Jeffrey Friedl's book [Fri97]. There's a lot of esoterica in there that won't be covered here. Instead, this chapter will give you a quick intro to the things you'll use most often. The first section introduces the basic elements of regular expressions. The sections that follow show how to extract matched data from strings and some of the things you can do with RE's more advanced features. The final section then shows how to do some of these things in other languages.

3.1 The Shell

A regular expression, or RE, is a pattern that can match strings of text. In languages such as C++, Java, and Python, REs are written as strings and processed by a library; in Perl, Ruby, and the Unix shell, REs are built right in.

Here's a simple example. When you type

```
rm *.java
```

at a shell prompt, the shell interprets *.java to mean "any filename ending in .java." This happens because the * is a *wildcard*, which the shell can match against any number of characters. If you typed

```
rm t*.java
```

the shell would delete today.java and tomorrow.java, but not yesterday.java, since it starts with a *y* rather than a *t*.

```
rm *t*
```

would delete anything with a *t* anywhere in its name, and of course the dreaded

```
rm *
```

would set your project back three months.[3] Note that the shell always matches each pattern against an *entire* string—the pattern *y*.java* doesn't match the file-name xyz.java.

All right, you know all of this. What you probably don't know is that most shells provide two other ways to match patterns. The first is *?,* which matches any single character. For example, this:

```
rm *.htm?
```

deletes files ending in .html but not those ending in .htm (nothing to match the *?*) or .htmxpro (too many characters to match the *?*). Similarly, this:

```
rm nov-0?.log
```

deletes files with names like nov-00.log and nov-07.log but leaves nov-12.log and nov-30.log alone.

The other bit of pattern matching built into the shell lets you match character sets. If you type

```
cp *.[Jj]ava /tmp
```

the shell copies all files whose names end in .java or .Java to the /tmp directory. It does *not* copy anything whose name ends in .Jjava: the square brackets mean "match exactly one of the enclosed characters."

If you want to match any character from a contiguous range, such as 0–9, you don't have to write them all out. Instead, you can do this:

```
cp version[0-9].txt /tmp
```

In this case, the pattern matches 0, 1, 2, and so on, up to 9. You can use other patterns, like *[a-z]* or *[A-Z]*, to match other character ranges.[4]

3.2 Basic Patterns

As you can see from the previous examples, every regular expression combines literal values (like *A* and *123*) and operators (like * and ?), just as arithmetic expressions combine numbers like 98.6 with + and /. We'll show regular expressions here by enclosing them in special symbols like this: ⌜regexp⌟ (the symbols are not part of the regular expression itself).

---

[3]Unless you were using a version control system, in which case it would set you back only three hours...

[4]But read Section 3.5, *Speaking in Tongues*, on page 69 first.

The rules for writing regular expressions in programming languages like Python and Java are a little different from those for writing them in the shell. For example, you can't write ⌜x*x⌟ to match things that begin and end with *x*; as you'll see in a second, that pattern means *a string consisting entirely of x's.*

Why the difference? The reason is that the rules used in programs are derived directly from the original mathematical notation, in which * was written as a superscript, as in a^*. The shell's rules, on the other hand, were designed to minimize typing in common cases, even if that meant that less common cases were harder (or impossible) to express.

The simplest way to explain how REs work in programs is probably by example:

⌜ab3⌟ matches *ab3*, but not *ab2*, *bc*, *AB3*, or *xyz*.
　　Each alphanumeric character matches itself. Matches are case-sensitive.

⌜a*⌟ matches the empty string, *a*, *aa*, etc., but not *b* or *A*.
　　An asterisk (*) means zero or more of whatever it follows. Anything followed by * can always match the empty string.

⌜b+⌟ matches *b*, *bb*, etc., but not the empty string.
　　A plus sign (+) means one or more of whatever it follows. An expression followed by + will match the empty string only if the expression itself would.

⌜ab?c⌟ matches *ac* or *abc*, but not *aXc*, *c*, *abbc*, or *acc*.
　　Whatever comes before ? is optional, i.e., it may appear zero or one times (but not more than once, which is why *abbc* isn't matched).

⌜a|b⌟ matches *a* or *b*, but not *ab* or the empty string.
　　A vertical bar (|) means "or"; it matches one or the other of its arguments, but not both.

⌜a|b|c|d⌟ matches *a*, *b*, *c*, or *d*, but not *ad* or the empty string.
　　Just as the + in arithmetic, | can be chained together.

⌜[abc]⌟ matches *a*, *b*, or *c*, but not *ab*, *cc*, or the empty string.
　　Square brackets ([]) denote a set of characters and match exactly one of its members; it's a shorthand for using | to combine several elements.

⌜[acgt]+|[ACGT]+⌟ matches *gattaca* and *ATGCATAG*, but not *aTcG* or *cCaGt*.
　　Any DNA sequence written entirely in lowercase or upper case.

⌜ab|cd⌟ matches *ab* or *cd*, but not *abd* or *acd*.
　　The "or" operator | has lower precedence than simply putting characters next to one another. It's exactly the same as in arithmetic, where 5x+3y means *5 times x, plus 3 times y,* rather than *5 times (x plus 3) times y.*

⌈a(b|c)d⌋ matches *abd* or *acd*, but not *ab*, *cd*, or *ad*.

> Parentheses can be used to override operator precedence, just as in arithmetic.

⌈a*(b|c)[xy]?⌋ matches *b*, *ac*, *aabx*, and so on.

> All of the previous operators can be combined with each other.

Two notational shorthands make REs much easier to write. The first is that . on its own matches any single character except newline.[5] The second is that you can indicate a range of characters in a set like ⌈[a-z]⌋, instead of having to spell them all out. Exactly what constitutes a "range" depends on the character set you're using (see Section 3.5, *Speaking in Tongues*, on page 69), but

- ⌈[a-z]⌋ matches lowercase letters,

- ⌈[A-Z]⌋ matches uppercase letters, and

- ⌈[0-9]⌋ matches digits.

You can also combine several ranges, along with single characters, in one set. The expression ⌈[A-Za-z]⌋, for example, matches a single alphabetic character, while ⌈[0-9,]+⌋ matches a nonempty sequence of digits and commas. This isn't quite the same as a longhand number, since it includes strings like *1,2,3*; we'll see a more complicated expression later that does this job.

Using just the operators we've seen so far, we can write a lot of useful patterns. The pattern ⌈gr[ae]y⌋, for example, matches both legal Canadian spellings of *gray* (or *grey*); the slightly more complex expression ⌈[Gg]r[ae]y⌋ matches both lowercase and title case versions. If we're searching through a list of filenames, ⌈.*java⌋ will match anything ending in the four letters *j*, *a*, *v*, *a* (remember, . on its own matches any single character, so ⌈.*⌋ matches any string of any length). And if we're trying to find hyperlinks in an HTML file, the expression ⌈<a href=".*">⌋ will catch most of them—most, not all, because

- it's legal to put more than one space between the opening <*a* and the *href*;
- both the *a* and the *href* could be in upper or mixed case; and
- if the link has any attributes after the *href*, such as
  <*a href="http://www.pragprog.com" rev="bibliography"*>
  then the regular expression will match everything from the opening quote of the *href* to the closing quote of the *rev*. This happens because matching is

---

[5]Why not newline? Because when REs were first introduced to programming languages, newline was the end-of-line marker, and programmers' lives were simpler if they didn't have to worry about accidentally matching it.

greedy, a subject I'll return to in Section 3.3, *Compilation and Reluctance*, on page 56.

Now, what if we want to match a literal * in a string? Or a *?*, or a *.*? In these cases, we have to *escape* the special character by putting a backslash in front of it. The RE ⌜a\.b⌟ matches exactly one string, *a.b*, nothing more, nothing less. Oh, and to match an backslash, we have to escape it too, so ⌜a\\b⌟ matches the three-character string *a\b*.

Using Regular Expressions in Programs

Right, so how do we actually use regular expressions? In Python, we import the regular expression library, re, and then use re.search(). The first argument to this function is the pattern we want to match; the second is the string we're trying to match it against.

For example, let's find all of the places where public classes are defined in a Java source file:

```
import sys, re
for filename in sys.argv[1:]:
    input = open(filename, 'r')
    for line in input:
        if re.search("public class", line):
            print "%s: %s" % (filename, line)
    input.close()
```

Not much different from searching for the substring, is it? But what if some programmers put tabs between the keywords *public* and *class*? (Yes, they're out there....) Let's use this:

```
import sys, re
pattern = "public[ \\t]+class"
for filename in sys.argv[1:]:
    input = open(filename, 'r')
    for line in input:
        if re.search(pattern, line):
            print "%s: %s" % (filename, line)
    input.close()
```

If you read *pattern* left to right, it says, "Match the string *public*, followed by one or more occurrences of any character from the set containing space and tab, followed by the word *class*."

Now, what about the words *abstract* and *synchronized*? We don't care if they appear before the word *public*, but they could also appear between it and *class*.

Let's take it a step at a time. *synchronized* or *abstract* is ⌜synchronized|abstract⌟. The RE to match *synchronized* optionally followed by *abstract*, with either spaces or tabs in between, is ⌜synchronized([\t]+abstract)?⌟. Of course, *abstract* could

Joe Asks...
Why the Double Backslashes?

Notice that the backslashes in the patterns have been doubled up. To understand why, you first have to understand that every regular expression you write in a Python program (or in C++ or Java) is parsed twice: once by the language and once by the regular expression library. Think about the string *a\nb*. When the Python parser sees this in a source file, it creates the string *a*, newline, *b*, because backslash is the language's own escape character. It then hands that three-character string—not the four-character sequence the user typed in but the three characters produced by parsing that sequence—to the regular expression library.

So, if we want *a\nb* to reach the RE library, we have to write it as *a\\nb*. If we want to match an actual backslash, we have to create the pattern ⌜\\⌟, which means we have to put four backslashes in the original string, like this: \ \ \ \.

Having to double up the backslashes is such a pain that some languages provide work-arounds. In Python, for example, you can write a *raw string* by prefixing it with the letter *r*, as in *r"x\ty"*. \ has no special meaning in a raw string, so *r"x\ty"* contains exactly the four characters you see, rather than an *x*, a tab, and a *b*.

Perl and Ruby go even further, and make regular expressions part of the language. As we'll see in Section 3.6, *Other Systems*, on page 71, you can write this in a Ruby program:

```
line =~ /public[ \t]+class/
```

to see whether *line* matches a pattern. Since the \ isn't inside a string, it doesn't need to be doubled.

come first, which would be ⌈abstract([\t]+synchronized)?⌋. If we want to accommodate both, we really should | these two together....

But why bother? We don't really care if someone has *public abstract abstract abstract class* in their Java; that's the compiler's problem, not ours. We can get away with saying, "The keyword *public*, followed by any number of occurrences of *abstract* or *synchronized*, followed by *class*." As the following program shows, that's a lot simpler to write:

```python
import sys, re
pattern = "public[ \\t]+((abstract|synchronized)[ \\t]+)*class"
for filename in sys.argv[1:]:
    input = open(filename, 'r')
    for line in input:
        if re.search(pattern, line):
            print "%s: %s" % (filename, line)
    input.close()
```

Some Example Patterns

Rather than stepping through examples of each of the operators in turn, let's try nine different patterns against each of nine different strings:

```python
import re
RE = ['',        'a',      'a.b',
      'a?b',     'a*b',    'a+b',
      'a\\.b',   'a\\+b', '.*ab']
data = ['',      'a',      'b',
        'Xab',   'aXb',    'abX',
        'ab',    'aXXXb', 'a.b']
# Tidy display
def show (s):
    if s is None:
        s = ""
    elif len(s) == 0:
        s = "''"
    print "%-6s" % s,
# Title
show(None)
for d in data:
    show(d)
print
# Results
for expr in RE:
    show(expr)
    for d in data:
        if re.search(expr, d):
            show("+")
        else:
            show("-")
    print
```

This program tries to match each of the regular expressions in *RE* against each of the strings in *data*, displaying + if the RE matches and - if it doesn't. Its output is

		a	b	Xab	aXb	abX	ab	aXXXb	a.b
	+	+	+	+	+	+	+	+	+
a	-	+	-	+	+	+	+	+	+
a.b	-	-	-	-	+	-	-	-	+
a?b	-	-	+	+	-	+	+	-	-
a*b	-	-	+	+	+	+	+	+	+
a+b	-	-	-	+	-	+	+	-	-
a\.b	-	-	-	-	-	-	-	-	+
a\+b	-	-	-	-	-	-	-	-	-
.*ab	-	-	-	+	-	+	+	-	-

A few observations are:

- The empty pattern (represented by an equally empty string) matches against everything since every string starts with the empty string (even the empty string itself).

- The pattern ⌜a⌟ matches anything that contains the letter *a* since re.search() tries to find a match *anywhere* in the target string. If you want to force the RE to match at the beginning of the string, use re.match() instead of re.search(), or read ahead to Section 3.3, *Extracting Matched Values*, on the following page to see how to anchor a match to the beginning or end of a string.

- We discussed ⌜a.b⌟ before. The pattern ⌜a?b⌟ means "an optional *a*, followed by a *b* that has to be there." It *doesn't* match the string *a* on its own (no terminating *b*), or *aXb* (the *a* and the *b* aren't adjacent).

- In this example, ⌜a*b⌟ matches the same strings as ⌜a?b⌟. If ⌜a*b⌟ was used with the string *aaaaaaaab*, though, it would match the entire string, while ⌜a?b⌟ would match only the last two characters. This is because matching is *greedy*, i.e., a regular expression matches the leftmost, longest sequence of characters it can. We'll talk about this more in Section 3.3, *Compilation and Reluctance*, on page 56.

- ⌜a+b⌟ matches the same strings as ⌜a*b⌟, except that ⌜a+b⌟ doesn't match *b* on its own, because + means "one or more," not "zero or more."

- The two patterns ⌜a\.b⌟ and ⌜a\+b⌟ match the strings *a.b* and *a+b*, respectively. Since only the first one is in the test data, the pattern ⌜a\+b⌟ doesn't match anything at all.

- Finally, ⌜.*ab⌟ means "zero or more characters followed by an adjacent *a* and *b*," which matches exactly what it's supposed to match.

Take a moment to understand why each pattern matches the strings it does and (just as importantly) why it *doesn't* match the other strings. While these examples are artificial, they are the basis for everything that follows.

Finally, if you prefer Java, the equivalent program is

```java
import java.util.regex.Pattern;
public class Pairs {
    private static final String RE[] = {
        "",        "a",       "a.b",
        "a?b",     "a*b",     "a+b",
        "a\\.b",  "a\\+b",  ".*ab"
    };
    private static final String _Data[] = {
        "",        "a",       "b",
        "Xab",     "aXb",     "abX",
        "ab",      "aXXXb",   "a.b"
    };
    // Tidy display
    private static void show(String s) {
        if (s == null) {
            s = "\t";
        }
        else if (s.trim().length() == 0) {
            s = "''";
        }
        System.out.print(s);
    }
    // Results
    public static void main(String[] args) {
        show(null);
        for (int j=0; j<_Data.length; ++j) {
            show("\t" + _Data[j]);
        }
        System.out.println();
        for (int i=0; i<RE.length; ++i) {
            String re = RE[i];
            show(re);
            for (int j=0; j<_Data.length; ++j) {
                String data = _Data[j];
                boolean m = Pattern.matches(re, data);
                show(m ? "\t+" : "\t-");
            }
            System.out.println();
        }
    }
}
```

3.3 Extracting Matched Values

It's all very well to know whether a pattern matched, but how do you find out *what* it matched? In the case of a literal pattern, like ⌜abc⌟, there can be no surprises, but if the pattern contains wildcards, like ⌜ab*c⌟, you will usually want to know how many times *b* appeared (if at all).

Every regular expression library therefore provides a way to recover the data that a pattern matched. If you put part of the regular expression in parentheses, the library remembers which part of the target string it matched against and can give

Matching vs. Searching

Some regular expression libraries (such as Python's) distinguish between matching and searching. *Matching* always lines the regular expression up with the start of the target string; *searching* looks for the RE anywhere in the target. This means that re.match(a.*, bat) fails (because *bat* doesn't start with an *a*), but re.search(a.*, bat) succeeds.

In order to avoid confusing myself, I never use re.match(). Instead, when I want to force the pattern to line up with the start of the target string, I anchor it using the special characters discussed in Section 3.3, *Extracting Matched Values*, on the facing page. Other languages, such as Java, avoid the problem entirely by providing only one method.

it to you later. It does this by returning a *match object*, whose methods let you ask questions about what happened during the match.

For example, the statement

```
m = re.search("a(b*)c", "_abbbbc_")
```

assigns a match object to *m*. The following expressions then have the values shown:

m.group(1)   *bbbb*   The text matching the first parenthesized group

m.start(1)   2   The index of the start of what matched the first group

m.end(1)   6   One past the end of what matched the first group

We can use this to build a list of the addresses of the people we've sent mail to recently. Assume that our outgoing messages have been stored in a file called sent.mbox. Each message looks like this:

```
From gvwilson@cs.utoronto.ca Mon Nov  1 06:01:22 2004 -0500
Date: Mon, 29 Nov 2004 06:01:22 -0500 (EST)
From: Greg Wilson <gvwilson@cs.utoronto.ca>
To: andy@pragprog.com
Subject: Re: Unicode characters
Message-ID: <Pine.GSO.4.58.0411010.1613@pterry.third-bit.com>
In-Reply-To: <1099289055.4185d1df90155@pragprog.com>
MIME-Version: 1.0
Content-Type: TEXT/PLAIN; charset=US-ASCII

p.s. a few Cyrillic characters would be cool, too, don't you think?

Thanks,
Greg
```

The addresses we want are on lines beginning with the string *To:*. No problem:

```
import sys, re
for line in sys.stdin:
    m = re.search("To: +(.+)", line)
    if m:
        print m.group(1)
```

As a quick test, we can run this on the single-message mailbox shown earlier:

```
andy@pragprog.com
<1099289055.4185d1df90155@pragprog.com>
```

Oops: we have to exclude lines beginning with *In-Reply-To:*. We *could* do this by matching everything with *To:* and then subtracting the lines we don't want, but there's a better way. If an RE begins with ^, it has to match at the start of the target string. The ^ is called an *anchor*; you can think of it as matching the spot before the string's first character. Similarly, if $ appears at the end of the RE, it anchors the match to the end of the target string.

Using this, our program is

```
import sys, re
for line in sys.stdin:
    m = re.search("^To: +(.+)$", line)
    if m:
        print m.group(1)
```

Rerun the test—yup, this does what we want. From here, we can use the techniques of the previous chapter to get rid of duplicates: put 'em in a dictionary, pipe the Python program's output through sort and uniq, and so on.

Example: Finding Email Addresses

Let's put this to work. Suppose we have an email archive, and we want to extract everything in it that looks like a valid email address so that we can sell them to direct-marketing companies—um, I mean, update our address book. Yes, that's it, update our address book. Anyway, we want to get the email addresses. How do we do it?

Real email addresses are a lot more complicated than most people think, but almost all addresses these days have the form *somebody@something.somewhere*. Each field can include letters, digits, and a few other characters like ., _, and -, but not characters like # or @ itself.

The regular expression that will match the characters allowed in an email address is therefore ⌈[a-zA-Z0-9_\.-]⌋. Notice that I've moved the - to the end of the set. If it's in the middle, the library thinks it's indicating a range and gets very confused. If it's at the beginning or the end, the library knows that it means itself. Notice

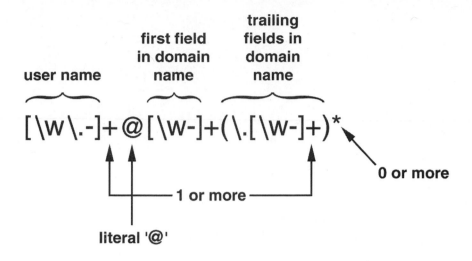

Figure 3.1: REGULAR EXPRESSION PARTS

also that I've written "match a dot" as ⌜\.⌟. When I translate this expression into a string in Python or Java, I'll have to double the backslash for the reasons discussed earlier.

Now, certain character sets are so common that the RE library provides a shorthand way to write them. The set of all digits, for example, can be written as ⌜\d⌟ (you'd have to write \\d in your program to produce a RE with a single backslash). Similarly, the set of whitespace characters (space, tab, carriage return, newline) is written ⌜\s⌟ (that's a lowercase *s*), and the set of "word" characters is written ⌜\w⌟. Of course, since regular expressions were invented by programmers, their idea of what's allowed in a word is a little strange; ⌜\w⌟ matches upper and lowercase letters, digits, and the underscore, which happen to be exactly those characters that are legal in C variable names.

All right, so what's a pattern to match email addresses? Let's try this:

```
[\w\.-]+@[\w-]+(\.[\w-]+)*
```

Looks like something you'd see if you opened a binary file in Notepad, doesn't it? But if you read it in pieces, from the inside out, it's actually not that bad (Figure 3.1).

Any regular expression more than a few characters long (and most short ones, too) should be tested before being trusted. After glancing at a couple of mail archives, the following seems like a good set of test cases:

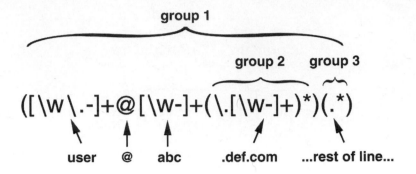

Figure 3.2: REGULAR EXPRESSION GROUPS

```
No address
Next line is blank

someone@somewhere.com
Line above matches at start, line below is indented:
        who@where.com
What about multiple matches?
first@first.com and second@second.com
What about dangling @ signs?
@nomatch.com
nomatch@  space after '@'
Let's try quotes: "a@b.com", <c@d.com>
And quotes in the middle: a'b@c.d
Longer domains with funny characters: p@q1.r-s.t_u
Short domains: x@y
```

In order, the valid email addresses in this file are

```
someone@somewhere.com
who@where.com
first@first.com
second@second.com
a@b.com
c@d.com
b@c.d
p@q1.r-s.t_u
x@y
```

Let's try this:[6]

```python
import sys, re
pattern = "([\\w.-]+@[\\w-]+(\\.[\\w-]+)*)"
for arg in sys.argv[1:]:
    input = open(arg, 'r')
```

---

[6]Notice that we don't need to escape the . in the character set with a backslash—inside square brackets, a period is just a period.

```
    for line in input:
        m = re.search(pattern, line)
        if m:
            address = m.group(1)
            print address
input.close()
```

Its output is

```
someone@somewhere.com
who@where.com
first@first.com
a@b.com
b@c.d
p@q1.r-s.t_u
x@y
```

Hmm...the two addresses *second@second.com* and *c@d.com* are both missing. They also happen to appear second on lines that contain other addresses. It looks like we need to do something to get all of the matches from a line, rather than just the first one.

The usual way to do this is to modify the regular expression to capture

- anything in front of the pattern we're interested in (which we discard),

- the first match for our pattern (which we keep), and

- everything after it (which we also keep).

Initialize a variable to the entire starting string, and enter a loop. On each pass through the loop, search the remaining data for the pattern. If it's found, extract the match, set the loop variable to whatever appears after that match, and go around again. This leaves us with

```
import sys, re
pattern = "([\\w.-]+@[\\w-]+(\\.[\\w-]+)*)(.*)"
for arg in sys.argv[1:]:
    input = open(arg, 'r')
    for line in input:
        while line:
            m = re.search(pattern, line)
            if m:
                address = m.group(1)
                remainder = m.group(3)
                print address
                line = remainder
            else:
                line = None
input.close()
```

Bingo—it prints all the valid addresses in the test data.[7]

---

[7]However, it still misses many valid addresses—see http://www.faqs.org/rfcs/rfc2821.html for the gory details.

Note that on each pass through the loop, we take the remainder from group 3, not group 2. Why? Because the second set of parentheses in the regular expression lies inside group 1's parentheses (Figure 3.2 on page 54).

This happens because parentheses always produce groups, even if they're in the expression only to control the scope of an operator. The RE library has no way of knowing which sets of parentheses you will think are important, so it's up to you to count them properly.[8]

Compilation and Reluctance

When we use re.search(pattern, text), the RE library translates the string *pattern* into a compiled regular expression object each time we call the function. We can make our program more efficient by having the library compile the pattern once and then reuse the compiled object. The code that does this is

```
import sys, re
patObj = re.compile("([\\w.-]+@[\\w-]+(\\.[\\w-]+)*)(.*)")
for arg in sys.argv[1:]:
    input = open(arg, 'r')
    for line in input:
        while line:
            m = patObj.search(line)
            if m:
                address = m.group(1)
                remainder = m.group(3)
                print address
                line = remainder
            else:
                line = None
    input.close()
```

We *must* compile the regular expression if we want to get at the data it matches in Java. We also have to create more objects to read data from files and explicitly handle exceptions, but the final result is still pretty readable:

```
import java.io.*;
import java.util.regex.*;
public class AllAddresses1 {
    String PatStr = "([\\w_\\.-]+@[\\w_-]+(\\.[\\w_-]+)*)(.*)";
    public static void main(String[] args) {
        try {
            Pattern patObj = Pattern.compile(PatStr);
            for (int i=0; i<args.length; ++i) {
                String filename = args[i];
                BufferedReader input =
                    new BufferedReader(new FileReader(filename));
```

---

[8]In most modern RE libraries, you can stop parentheses from creating groups by putting ?: immediately after the opening parenthesis. For example, while ⌜(a)(b)(c)⌝ has three groups, ⌜(a)(?:b)(c)⌝ has only two. I find this hard to read, so I always just count off groups from left to right.

```
            String line;
            while ((line = input.readLine()) != null) {
                while (line.length() > 0) {
                    Matcher m = patObj.matcher(line);
                    if (m.matches()) {
                        System.out.println(m.group(1));
                        line = m.group(3);
                    }
                    else {
                        break;
                    }
                }
            }
        }
        catch (FileNotFoundException e) {
            System.err.println("No such file: " + e);
        }
        catch (IOException e) {
            System.err.println("Error reading line: " + e);
        }
    }
}
```

Compile it, test it by running it against the same data file we used to test the Python program, and the output is

```
someone@somewhere.com
first@first.com
```

Uh, what? Why is it only finding two addresses? Well, Java insists that regular expressions must match the front of the target string (just like Python's re.match() function). Any addresses that are embedded in other text are missed.

All right, that's simple enough to fix. We know that ⌜.*⌟ will match any sequence of characters, including the empty string. Let's put it at the front of the regular expression like this:

```
String PatStr = ".*([\\w\\.-]+@[\\w-]+(\\.[\\w-]+)*)(.*)";
```

Compile it, run it, and we get

```
e@somewhere.com
o@where.com
d@second.com
c@d.com
b@c.d
p@q1.r-s.t_u
x@y
```

That's not right either: it's throwing away everything in the string except the first character before the @, including any email addresses that happen to match before the last one.

What's happening is that regular expressions are *greedy* by default. In other *greedy* words, they try to match as much text as possible, as early as possible, while still

Regular Expression Iteration

Some languages provide a way to iterate through all matches to a regular expression so that you don't have to write the "match, strip, and repeat" loop yourself. For example, Python's regular expressions have a method called finditer(), which creates an iterator that returns each non-overlapping match for a regular expression in turn. This allows you to write more readable code such as

```
for address in re.finditer("([\\w.-]+@[\\w-]+(\\.[\\w-]+)*)"):
    print address
```

In Java, the Matcher class's find() method attempts to find the next subsequence of the input string that matches the pattern. When called repeatedly, it returns successive matches one after another.

matching everything. Our regular expression says that there has to be at least one character before the @ sign; when we give the RE a string like *fred@abc.com*, the ⌜.*⌟ can match the letters *fre* and still leave *d@abc.com* for the rest of the RE. And when we have multiple addresses in a string, all but the last are eaten by the ⌜.*⌟.

The solution is to make the ⌜.*⌟ at the front of the regular expression *reluctant*, rather than greedy, so that it will match as few characters as possible, rather than as many. The three operators *?*, ***, and *+* all have reluctant forms, which are spelled *??*,**?*, and *+?*. For example, ⌜.*?⌟ matches the shortest string of zero or more characters that leaves enough data for the rest of the RE to match, rather than the longest. Make this one-character change to the pattern string in the Java program, so that it is

```
String PatStr = ".*?([\\w\\.-]+@[\\w-]+(\\.[\\w-]+)*)(.*)";
```

and voila, the output now matches the same nine addresses that the Python program found.

Making Expressions Readable

This is great—we're finding and extracting email addresses in just a few lines of code, without having to parse all the different forms ourselves. When it comes time to modify the program, though, we may have to pay back all the time we've saved, with interest, just trying to understand the regular expression we wrote. For this reason, it's always a good idea to break REs into pieces and comment each piece. One way to do this is to build the RE by adding commented strings together, like this:

```
String patStr =
      ".*?"                    // anything before the first address
    + "("                      // start of group 1
    + "[\\w_\\.-]+"            // user name
    + "@"                      // literal '@'
    + "[\\w_-]+"               // first part of domain
    + "(\\.[\\w_-]+)*"         // rest of domain (group 2)
    + ")"                      // end of group 1
    + "(.*)";                  // rest of string (group 3)
```

A better way is to embed the comments in the regular expression:

```
String patStr =
      ".*?                     # anything before the first address\n"
    + "(                       # start of group 1\n"
    + "[\\w_\\.-]+             # user name\n"
    + "@                       # literal '@'\n"
    + "[\\w_-]+                # first part of domain\n"
    + "(\\.[\\w_-]+)*          # rest of domain (group 2)\n"
    + ")                       # end of group 1\n"
    + "(.*)                    # rest of string (group 3)";
Pattern patObj = Pattern.compile(patStr, Pattern.COMMENTS);
```

Note that when the last example is compiled, we pass the flag *Pattern.COMMENTS*. This tells the RE library that everything from # to the end of the line inside the RE is a comment and that extra whitespace is to be ignored. (In Java, we have to provide the end-of-line character \n ourselves; in Python, we can use multiline strings.)

Other flags turn on case-insensitive matching, make . match newline characters (which it normally doesn't), and so on; see your language's documentation for the full list.

In Python, I often assign common subpatterns to variables and then create the full pattern by adding them together, like this:

```
prefix = ".*?"
user   = "[\\w\\.-]+"
domain = "[\\w-]+"
suffix = "(.*)"
patStr = prefix + "(" +
             user + "@" + domain + "(\\." + domain + ")*" +
         ")" + suffix
```

As the Perl folks are fond of saying, there's more than one way to do it.

3.4 Practical Applications

Let's put regular expressions through their paces.

> ### ⚡ Joe Asks...
> #### Do I Have to Figure All of This Out for Myself?
>
> Nope. There are several catalogs of regular expressions online, such as the one at `http://regexlib.com`. There are also several good free tools for building and debugging regular expressions; my favorites are Edi Weitz's Regex Coach (`http://weitz.de/regex-coach`), JRegexpTester (`http://jregexptester.sourceforge.net`), and the Rx Toolkit that comes with ActiveState's Komodo IDE (`http://www.activestate.com/Products/Komodo`).

Canadian Postal Codes

Canadian postal consist of six alternating letters and digits. My postal code, for example, is *M5T 2P4*; my government's is *K1A 0S5*, which is also sometimes written without the space as *K1A0S5*, and Santa Claus's is *H0H 0H0*. Here's a pattern that'll match either form:

```
[A-Z]\d[A-Z] ?\d[A-Z]\d
```

Each instance of ⌜[A-Z]⌟ matches exactly one uppercase letter (since there's no trailing *, +, or ? to modify it). Each ⌜\d⌟ matches a digit, and ? (space followed by question mark) matches one space, or nothing at all.

Times

That was too easy; let's try something more difficult. How about times on a 24-hour clock, like 08:43 or 21:27? The colon and what comes after it is just ⌜:[0-5][0-9]⌟, since minutes can take on any value from 00 to 59.

Getting the hours right is a little more complex. It's tempting to use ⌜[0-2][0-9]⌟, but that would allow times like 27:00, which don't exist. So break it down a little further: if the first digit of the hours is 0 or 1, the second digit can be anything from 0 to 9. On the other hand, if the first digit of the hours is 2, the second digit can only be 0, 1, 2, or 3. The first possibility is ⌜[01][0-9]⌟, and the second is ⌜2[0-3]⌟. Combine them with |, tack on the minutes, and the result is

```
([01][0-9]|2[0-3]):[0-5][0-9]
```

or equivalently

```
([01]\d|2[0-3]):[0-5]\d
```

(I'd probably actually write it the first way, since I think it's more readable, but there's no real difference between the two.)

Feet and Inches

How about a carpenter's shorthand for feet and inches? We want to match all of these:

5'   five feet
5'-3"   five feet, three inches
5'3"   the same, without the dash
3"   three inches

but none of these:

5   No feet or inches marker
5'3   Missing inches marker
5-3   Missing both markers
5-3"   Missing one marker

Just to make it interesting, let's disallow leading zeroes, so that measurements like 05'07" aren't matched either. The pattern is:

```
^([1-9]\d*')?-?([1-9]\d*")?$
```

Taking it apart, there are four pieces:

- The anchors ⌜^⌟ and ⌜$⌟ force the pattern to match the entire input string. Without this, the pattern would always match strings like *5'3*, since the first two characters are a legal measurement (five feet).

- ⌜([1-9]\d*')?⌟, matches an integer with a nonzero first digit, followed by a single quote. The *?* makes this optional, so we can match inches alone.

- The middle subexpression, ⌜-?⌟, will match a single dash if one is present.

- The third subexpression is just like the first, with a double quote instead of a single quote to indicate inches.

The subexpression ⌜[1-9]\d*⌟ is an example of a fairly common pattern: we want to match some set of characters in general, but a smaller set at the start. If we wanted to match title case words, like *Hello* and *Ruby*, we would use:

```
[A-Z][a-zA-Z]*
```

But wait a second. Wait just one pattern-matching second. All three of the subexpressions in the "solution" above are optional, so this pattern would also match the empty string. What's worse, if the first (feet) and last (inches) parts are empty, it also matches a single dash on its own, which definitely *isn't* a legal measurement.

The solution uses another pattern that crops up fairly often when writing REs. We want to allow each part of the RE to match the empty string, without allowing the entire RE to do so. The only general solution is to repeat part of the pattern, like this:

```
^([1-9]\\d*'|([1-9]\\d*'-?)?[1-9]\\d*\")$
```

The key to understanding this complex expression is the | in the middle, which matches either what's on its left or what's on its right. What's on the left matches only against feet, not inches; it will take care of 5' for us. What's on the right matches against something like 5' only if it's followed by a dash, and *always* matches against inches. This part of the expression handles both 5'-3" and 3" on its own, without allowing either a lonely dash or the empty string.

Exactly the same idea is used in this expression, which matches decimal numbers like 1.23 and .45, without matching a single . or the empty string:

```
([1-9]\d*)|([1-9]\d*\.)[1-9]\d*
```

Word Frequency

Let's take a look at a classic problem: building a histogram of how frequently different words appear in a document. As far as we're concerned, a word is a sequence of alphabetic characters, possibly including an apostrophe or dash, like *its*, *it's*, or *re-backburnerize*. We do *not* want to count things that look like code fragments, such as *abc123* or *this_file*, and we don't want to include punctuation that might directly abut a word, like the period after the end of this sentence.

Another feature of REs will help us out: ⌜\b⌟. This escape sequence doesn't match any characters. Instead, it matches the zero-width break between word and non-word characters (just as ^ matches the start of a string, and $ matches the end). For example, the expression ⌜.*\b(\d+)\b.*⌟ matches the string *the number 42*, and sets group 1 to *42*. The two occurrences of ⌜\b⌟ match between the space and the *4* and between the *2* and the comma, respectively.

Our program has two sections. The first extracts the words from the input and counts how often each occurs:

```
pat = re.compile("^.*?\\b([A-Za-z'-]+)\\b(.*)$")
concord = {}
for line in sys.stdin:
    m = pat.search(line)
    while m:
        word = m.group(1)
        concord[word] = concord.get(word, 0) + 1
        m = pat.search(m.group(2))
```

The second part gets a list of key/value pairs from the dictionary built by the first part and sorts it in descending order of frequency:

```
entries = concord.items()
entries = [(count, word) for (word, count) in entries]
entries.sort()
entries.reverse()
for (count, word) in entries:
    print "%6d\t%s" % (count, word)
```

The output isn't exactly what a human being would produce—it contains the string —*but*, for example, because I use a triple hyphen in my XML to indicate a long dash, like the one I'm about to type—but it's a good start.

Reformatting an Address List

Suppose you have a file containing names and email addresses, separated by one or more tabs:

```
Alan Turing             alan@cambridge.ac.uk
John von Neumann        johnny@ias.princeton.edu
Grace Hopper            ghopper@navy.mil
```

You want to reformat the list so that it looks like this:

```
"Alan Turing" <alan@cambridge.ac.uk>
"John von Neumann" <johnny@ias.princeton.edu>
"Grace Hopper" <ghopper@navy.mil>
```

The solution (in Python) is

```
import sys, re
pat = re.compile("([^\\t]+)\\t+(.+)")
for line in sys.stdin:
    m = pat.match(line.strip())
    name, email = m.group(1), m.group(2)
    print "\"%s\" <%s>" % (name, email)
```

Let's take it a step at a time:

1. The string *"([^\\t]+)\\t+(.+)"* in the source code creates the regular expression ⌜([^\t]+)\t*(.+)⌟ (because the double backslashes in the string are translated by the Python interpreter).

2. ⌜[^\t]⌟ means "anything that *doesn't* match a tab." In general, we can negate any character set by making ^ the first character inside the []. For example, the RE ⌜[^aeiou]⌟ means "any character that *isn't* a lowercase vowel." However, if ^ isn't the first character inside the square brackets, it just stands for itself: ⌜[v^]⌟ means "either a *v*, or a ^."

3. The parentheses around ⌜[^\t]⌟ tell the regular expression library to capture whatever it matches. Since these are the first parentheses, what matches becomes group 1.

4. The next part of the expression, ⌜\t+⌟, matches one or more tab characters.

5. Finally, ⌜(.+)⌟ matches everything after the tabs, up to the end of the line, and remembers it as group 2.

One other thing worth noting about this program is that it strips leading and trailing whitespace off the line before matching against it. Doing this makes our regular expression simpler, since it doesn't have to worry about (for example) blanks appearing after the email address.

Detecting Duplicated Words

One of the the most common mistakes people make with word processors is to duplicate duplicate words when cutting and pasting. Finding them on a single line uses a feature of regular expressions we haven't seen before: backward matches.

Suppose that instead of finding duplicated words, we wanted to find duplicated letters, like *aa* and *XX*. The pattern ⌜[a-zA-Z][a-zA-Z]⌟ wouldn't do it, since the first character set could match *p*, and the second one, *q*. This pattern will do the trick:

```
([a-zA-Z])\1
```

We've seen the first part before: match any single alphabetic character, and remember it. The *back-reference*⌜\1⌟ then tells the regular expression library to match whatever literal text the first parenthesized expression has *already* matched. If the first letter was *j*, for example, then ⌜\1⌟ would have to match a *j* as well in order for the pattern as a whole to match.

So, here's a program to match duplicated letters:

```
import sys, re
pat = re.compile(".*?(([a-zA-Z])\\2)(.*)")
for line in sys.stdin:
    m = pat.match(line)
    while m:
        paired, line = m.group(1), m.group(3)
        print paired
        m = pat.match(line)
```

1. ⌜.*?⌟ matches as few characters at the start of the target string as it can while still leaving enough for the rest of the pattern to match. If we just used ⌜.*⌟, we would only get the last match on any given line.

2. ⌜(([a-zA-Z])\2)⌟ matches and remembers doubled characters. So why is it ⌜\2⌟, instead of ⌜\1⌟? This is because parentheses are always counted from the left. We have one set around the character range ⌜[a-zA-Z]⌟, and another around the pair as a whole; counting from left to right, the parentheses around the character set are the *second* set.

3. As usual, the ⌜(.*)⌟ at the end matches and remembers everything else on the line so that we can search it for more matches.

All right, what about doubled words? The pattern is almost the same; all we have to do is

- allow more multiple characters in the first part of the match, instead of just one; and

- allow for space between the words.

```
import sys, re
pat = re.compile(".*?\\b(([a-zA-Z]+)\\s+\\2)(.*)")
for line in sys.stdin:
    m = pat.match(line)
    while m:
        paired, line = m.group(1), m.group(3)
        print "%s" % paired
        m = pat.match(line)
```

Note the ⌜\b⌝ before the start of the pattern that matches doubled words. Without this, the pattern would match the *is is* in *This is*, since it would be allowed to match within words. Note also that ⌜\s+⌝ (which matches spaces between words) is outside the innermost parentheses. If the pattern was

```
(([a-zA-Z]+\s+)\2)
```

then the ⌜\2⌝ would have to match the spaces after the first word, as well as the word itself. This would prevent it matching strings like *hello hello,* since the space after the first *hello* doesn't match the comma after the second.

One more refinement. Suppose the words are on different lines, as in

```
This is
is an example.
```

How do we match this? In both Python and Java, we put the entire input into a single string and then compile the regular expression with the *DOTALL* flag,[9] which tells the library that . is allowed to match newline characters (which it normally won't do):

```
import sys, re
pat = re.compile(".*?\\b(([a-zA-Z]+)\\s+\\2)(.*)", re.DOTALL)
data = sys.stdin.read()
m = pat.match(data)
while m:
    paired, data = m.group(1), m.group(3)
    print "%s" % paired
    m = pat.match(data)
```

Matching IP Addresses

A "raw" IP address is four sets of numbers, such as *109.27.43.3*. Each number will fit into a single unsigned byte (in other words, is in the range 0–255). We *could* match each field like this:

```
\d\d?\d?
```

---

[9]In Java, the flag is *java.util.regex.Pattern.DOTALL*.

but it's easier to express the "once, twice, or three times" constraint like this:

```
\d{1,3}
```

The numbers in curly braces tell the library the minimum and maximum number of matches allowed—in this case, at least one, and at most three. Our whole expression is then

```
\d{1,3}\.\d{1,3}\.\d{1,3}\.\d{1,3}
```

or, even more succinctly:

```
\d{1,3}(\.\d{1,3}){3}
```

since *{3}* matches exactly three instances of the pattern that comes before it.

It's important to note that this pattern also matches some dotted quads, like *999.999.999.999*, which are not legal IP addresses. It is possible to write an RE that matches only legal ones, but it's frighteningly complex. As powerful as they are, REs are not the solution to every problem; if you find yourself writing a ten-line RE, it may be time to look at some other solution. In this case, the solution is to break the matched text into groups and make sure that the integer value of each group is no greater than 255:

```python
import sys, re
pat = re.compile("(\\d{1,3})\\.(\\d{1,3})\\.(\\d{1,3})\\.(\\d{1,3})")
def validIp(text):
    try:
        m = pat.match(text)
        for g in m.groups():
            val = int(g)
            if val > 127:
                return False
        return True
    except:
        return False
for line in sys.stdin:
    line = line.strip()
    print line, "=>", validIp(line)
```

Removing HTML Tags

Suppose you want to remove all the HTML tags in a block of text so that you can run it through a speling checkr. It turns out that most regular expression libraries provide replacement, as well as search. For example, the following Python program replaces all occurrences of *big* with *little*; thanks to the \b's on either side of the word ⌈big⌉, it does this without turning *biggest* into *littlegest*:

```python
import sys, re
pat = re.compile("\\bbig\\b")
for line in sys.stdin:
    line = pat.sub("little", line.rstrip())
    print line
```

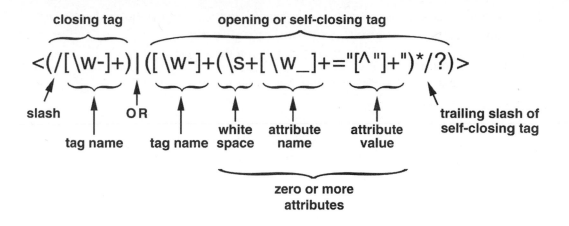

Figure 3.3: MATCHING HTML TAGS

All we have to do is come up with a pattern that matches HTML tags. Let's see: opening <, followed by letters and digits, followed by attributes (assume they're quoted for now), followed by a closing >. Oh, but if it's a closing tag, it'll be an opening <, a slash, the tag name, and a closing >, without attributes.

Once more, we're faced with the problem of long-distance dependencies: if there's a slash at the start of the tag, it can't have attributes, but if there's no slash, it can. And once again, the only way to solve the problem is case by case (Figure 3.3).

Phone Numbers

Finally, let's return to where we started: phone numbers. If we allow only spaces— no parentheses, no dashes—then the expression we want is

```
[2-9]\d{2} [1-9]\d{2} \d{3}
```

(We can't use ⌈\d{3}⌋ for the first letters of the first and second groups because area codes can't start with 0 or 1, and exchanges can't start with 0.)

Now, how about allowing parentheses around the area code?

```
[1-9]\d{2}|\([1-9]\d{2}\) [1-9]\d{2} \d{3}
```

Yup—we have to do it as an either/or if we want to stop ourselves from accepting numbers with only one parenthesis.

How about making the area code optional?

```
(([1-9]\d{2}|\([1-9]\d{2}\)) )?[1-9]\d{2} \d{3}
```

We have to remember to put the space separating the area code from the rest of the number inside the parentheses that surround the two options for the area code so that the space is allowed only if an area code is present.

How about a dash in between the last two parts of the number?

```
(([1-9]\d{2}|\([1-9]\d{2}\)) )?[1-9]\d{2}( |-)\d{3}
```

And so on. The end result may be fairly complex, but if you build it, and test it, in stages, it's a lot simpler than writing a function of your own to do the same job.

It'll probably run faster, too. Regular expression libraries have been studied and tuned by several generations of programmers. If you're doing anything more complex than looking for the first nonblank character in a line, the odds are pretty good that an RE will run faster than any code you could write by hand. This is especially true in languages such as Java and Python, since in most cases, the core of the RE library is coded in a lower-level language such as C.

There's another way to tackle this problem (there's *always* another way to tackle data crunching problems). Instead of trying to account for everything the user enters, we could just strip out everything that doesn't look like part of a phone number and then parse what's left.

It just so happens that regular expressions can be used to replace things, as well as match them. In Python, for example, RE objects have a method sub(), which replaces everything that matches the RE with a constant string. We can use this to strip all the whitespace, parentheses, and dashes out of the phone number and then match what's left against a 3-3-4 digit pattern:

```python
import sys, re
patStrip = re.compile("[\\(\\)\\s-]")
patPhone = re.compile("(\\d{3})(\\d{3})(\\d{4})")

tests = [
    "123 456 7890",
    "(123) 456-7890",
    "123-456 7890",
    "1 2 3 4 5 6 7 8 9 0"
]
for t in tests:
    print t
    temp = patStrip.sub("", t)
    m = patPhone.match(temp)
    assert len(m.groups()) == 3
    assert m.group(1) == "123"
    assert m.group(2) == "456"
    assert m.group(3) == "7890"
```

As you can see, this approach has its drawbacks too: the last string in the test set doesn't really look much like a phone number but meets our criteria.

3.5 Speaking in Tongues

Do you speak Thai? Or Russian, or Spanish? If you're doing business on the Internet, the odds are that at least a few of your potential customers do. If your web site falls over when they try to type in their name and address, they're probably going to take their business elsewhere.

To understand what this means for regular expressions, and data crunching in general, we have to take a detour through history.

Character Encoding

In the beginning (well, forty years ago), there was ASCII, the American Standard Code for Information Interchange. ASCII specified which character every 7-bit number mapped to: 63 meant *?*, for example, while 65 meant *A*, and 122 meant *z*. A few integers represented nonprinting control characters: 10 was newline, 13 was carriage return, and 7 made the bell ring.

Unfortunately, the ASCII character set didn't include é, ç, and other accented characters. It also didn't include ®, ß, Φ, θ, or any of the other zillions of symbols humanity expresses itself with. A later standard called ISO-8859-1 (often referred to as Latin-1) added enough of these to ASCII to fill a full 8 bits (256 characters), but that still left 99.999...% of characters out in the cold.

Enter Unicode. Unlike earlier standards, Unicode separated *logical encoding* from *physical encoding*. Logically, every character in every alphabet the Unicode committee cared about is represented by a unique *code point*, which is just a positive integer. The first 256 code points represent the same characters as Latin-1; higher code points represent characters that Latin-1 left out. Code points are typically written in hexadecimal with a *U+* prefix so that *U+010C* is a C with a caron (Č), while *U+05d0* is a Hebrew alef, א.

So how are code points represented? Programmers could use 16 bits per character instead of 8—except that even 65,536 characters isn't enough to include all of the East Asian alphabets, ancient Egyptian hieroglyphics, Mayan, and so on. How about 24 bits? Or 32? Well, 32 would be enough, but it would waste a lot of memory and disk space, since in practice, most data actually *does* fit into 8 bits. Quadrupling the size required to store your address book probably wouldn't matter, but quadrupling Google's disk requirements? That's real money.

As always, the solution is a compromise. Instead of encoding every character in the same number of bits, formats like UTF-8 (Unicode Transformation Format-8) use *variable-length encoding*. UTF-8 works as follows:

- Bytes in the range 0–255 (hex 0000–007F) represent the same characters that they did in ASCII. As bit strings, these bytes all have the form 0xxxxxxx.

- Code points from 128 to 2047 (hex 0080–07FF) use two bytes in the form 110xxxxx 10xxxxxx.

- Code points from there up to 65535 ($2^{16}-1$) use three bytes of the form 1110xxxx 10xxxxxx 10xxxxxx, and so on.

The best thing about this scheme is that the original 7-bit ASCII characters are stored as they always were. The worst thing is that different logical characters now have very different physical lengths. You can no longer just count bytes in memory to figure out how long a string is; you have to walk it from start to end, decoding as you go.

Now, if everything was encoded using UTF-8, life would be good. However, Unicode can also be encoded using UTF-16 (most characters represented in two bytes, the rest in four), or using UCS-4 (all characters in four bytes), or using any of the dozens of pre-Unicode "legacy" encodings for Greek, Hebrew, Japanese (there are at least three), and so on. The result is that *there's no such thing as "plain" text*. If you don't know what physical encoding was used for a string, you absolutely, positively cannot interpret the string's content.

So how do programs tell how strings are encoded? Browsers do it by looking for the following at the start of HTML pages:

```
<html>
<head>
<meta http-equiv="Content-Type" content="text/html; charset=utf-8"/>
```

This works because just about every encoding on the planet maps the first 255 bytes to the old ASCII characters, so the browser can (almost) always read this much of a document without trouble.

Unicode and Regular Expressions

What does all of this imply for regular expressions? The first thing it means is that if you're handling international data, you have to read your language's documentation very, very carefully. When it tells you that . matches a single character, does it really mean "a single logical character," or "a single byte"? If your string is Hiragana, encoded using UTF-8, a . on its own might match only the first physical byte of the three needed to represent an actual (logical) character.

Let's throw a few more onions in the stew. For what probably seemed like good reasons at the time, Unicode allows some characters to be represented in more than one way. For example, à is either U+00E0 *or* the two-character sequence

U+0061 (lowercase *a*) followed by U+0300 (grave accent). Then there's the question of case: the uppercase Greek sigma Σ has two lowercase equivalents, *σ* and ς, while the uppercase version of the German *ß* is *SS*, and so on. Does your regular expression library do the right thing with these when you ask it to do a case-insensitive match? If so, does it work correctly for all alphabets or just for a handful of common European ones?

The right way to handle all of this is to rely on *scripts*, *blocks*, and *categories*. As its name suggests, a script is a set of characters used in a particular language; the Cyrillic script, for example, includes all the characters used to write Russian.

Blocks are similar but are guaranteed to be contiguous range of values; U+0000 to U+007F is the Basic Latin block, U+0400 to U+04FF is the Cyrillic block, and U+3040 to U+309F is the Hiragana block. Blocks aren't as robust as scripts—the Currency block, for example, doesn't include the dollar sign—but they're simpler to implement, so they're more widely available.

Categories are more conceptual in nature: the category *Lu* means "uppercase characters in any alphabet," while *Pi* is the set of all initial quotes, and *Pf* is the set of all final (closing) quotes.

Java and Perl programmers represent Unicode blocks using ⌜\p{InWhatever}⌟, so ⌜\p{InCyrillic}⌟ matches any single Cyrillic character. Categories use *Is* instead of *In*: ⌜\p{IsLu}⌟ matches a single uppercase letter from any alphabet. Meanings can be negated by using an uppercase *P* instead of a lowercase one: ⌜\P{IsLu}⌟ matches any character that *isn't* uppercase.

The website at `http://www.fileformat.info/info/unicode/` describes all of the scripts, blocks, and categories you're every likely to need. In practice, though, it's usually easier to find what you want in the documentation for your language's regular expression library, especially if you're using Perl.

3.6 Other Systems

Regular expressions are so useful that they're built into many widely used tools. The shell is one; to end this chapter, we'll take a look at some others: a Unix tool called grep and a couple of alternatives to Python.

Grep

Searching a file line by line to find matches for a regular expression is such a common operation that one of the standard Unix tools, called grep, does nothing

[:alnum:]	Alphanumeric characters (*[:alpha:]* plus *[:digit:]*)
[:alpha:]	Alphabetic characters (*[:lower:]* and *[:upper:]*)
[:blank:]	Space and tab
[:cntrl:]	Control characters, like carriage return, newline, and bell
[:digit:]	The digits 0–9
[:graph:]	"Graphical" characters (*[:alnum:]* and *[:punct:]*)
[:lower:]	The lowercase letters a–z
[:print:]	Printable characters (*[:alnum:]*, *[:punct:]*, and space)
[:punct:]	The punctuation characters ! "#$%&'()*+,-./:;<=>?@[\]^_{|}~
[:space:]	The whitespace characters (tab, newline, space, etc.)
[:upper:]	The uppercase letters A–Z
[:xdigit:]	The hexadecimal digits 0–9, A–F, and a–f

Figure 3.4: GREP CHARACTER SETS

else.[10,11] The grep command takes a regular expression as a command-line argument, and prints out lines from its input that match that expression. To find all uses of the word *payment* in a set of mailboxes, for example, you can either do this:

```
grep payment *.mbox
```

or this:

```
cat *.mbox | grep payment
```

The second command works because grep reads from standard input if no file-names are given (just like all well-behaved Unix commands).

grep's regular expressions follow almost exactly the same rules as the ones we've already seen. ., ?, *, +, and *[]* do what you (should now) expect. So do ⌜\w⌟ and ⌜\b⌟, but most other character sets are written inside square brackets as shown in Figure 3.4.

There's a lot more to grep, too. The anchors ^ and $ do the right thing, back-references like ⌜\1⌟ work, and so on. In practice, though, I find that if I need to do something this complicated, I probably need other things as well, such as functions and data structures, so I've probably left grep behind and am writing Python.

---

[10]The name grep isn't actually an acronym for anything. Instead, the name comes from a command in the Unix text editor ed that took the form g/re/p, meaning, "search globally for matches to the regular expression *re*, and *print* lines where they are found." Obvious, really...

[11]You can tell a programmer's age by whether she uses grep or google to mean, "to search for."

Perl, Ruby, and All That

Ah, Perl...What can I say about it that hasn't been said a thousand times before? What words can possibly capture its unique mix of utility and unreadability? What invective can I heap upon its tangled, yet ever-so-useful, head?

None, probably, so I'll move on to Ruby. In case you haven't seen it, it has all of the good features of Perl, with few or none of its warts. In particular, regular expressions are built into the language, as are a few special operators for finding matches and extracting matched text.

Here's a simple example:

```
re = /(\d+):(\d+)/
md = re.match("It is now 9:30 am")
print md.class, "\n"
print md[0], "\n"
print md[1], "\n"
print md[2], "\n"
print "'" + md.pre_match + "'\n"
print "'" + md.post_match + "'\n"
```

It prints

```
MatchData
9:30
9
30
'It is now '
' am'
```

All you have to do to create an RE is put the pattern inside forward slashes.[12] Since this isn't a string, you don't have to double up any backslashes (although you obviously do have to escape any forward slashes—life is never perfect). After that, everything looks pretty much like it does in Python.

But now look at this:

```
re = /(\d+):(\d+)/
md = re.match("It is now 9:30 am")
print md.class, "\n"
print $&, "\n"
print $1, "\n"
print $2, "\n"
print "'" + $` + "'\n"
print "'" + $' + "'\n"
```

It does exactly the same thing as the previous program using special variables built into the language. $& means "everything that matched the last time a regular expression was used"; $1, $2, and so on are any groups from that match, while $` and $' are whatever came before and after the match, respectively.

---

[12]You can also use balanced delimiters, as in %r{(\d+):(\d+)} or %r{/(\d+):(\d+)}. I usually don't, because I keep losing track of which []s and {}s are delimiters and which are part of the RE.

But wait, there's more. Ruby uses the matching operator =~ to match strings against regular expressions, so

```
/e(\w+)i/ =~ "something"
```

leaves *th* in group 1. The actual result of =~ is the index of the start of the match between the RE and the string, so that

```
loc = "something" =~ /e(\w+)i/
```

assigns 3 to *loc*.

You can even use a regular expression to drive a loop so that you don't have to match, extract, and repeat, as in Section 3.3, *Example: Finding Email Addresses*, on page 52:

```
line.scan(/([\w.-]+@[\w-]+(\.[\w-]+)*)/) { |addr| puts addr[0] }
```

So, is language-level support for regular expressions a good thing or not? =~ is easier to write (and read) than Python's pat.match(). On the other hand, if you're going to add an operator to the language for matching, why not add one for substitution, as well? And how about max and min? They're perfectly sensible binary operators; why not write them as *a<?b* and *a>?b*? And—

But no. No, no, no. That way lies madness.[13] At some point, you have to stop adding support for special cases and start providing programmers with ways to extend the language themselves. Which side of that boundary you think =~ lies on is largely a matter of taste; what's important is whether the code you write can be read by someone else once you've left the building.

3.7 Summary

Regular expressions are one of the most widely used data crunching tools around. Yes, they're hard to read (even if you add comments), but they make a lot of things possible that would otherwise be too hard to be worth tackling.

Here are a few things to keep in mind as you start working with REs:

- Build your expression up piece by piece, rather than trying to write the whole thing in one go, and test as you go along.

- If your library uses different functions for matching only at the beginning of the string and for matching anywhere, make sure you use the right one.

- If you want to extract every match, and you don't know how many there are, write a loop that breaks the input into three pieces—stuff before the first

---

[13]See http://www.ozonehouse.com/mark/blog/code/PeriodicTable.html for proof.

match, the match itself, and stuff after—and keep running it until you fail to find a match.

- Remember the difference between greedy and reluctant matching, and make sure you use the right one.

- Use character classes, even if your data doesn't contain non-ASCII characters (because sooner or later, it will).

- Most important, don't try to be too clever. Remember: regular expressions aren't the only tool you have, and you don't have to do everything in a single RE (any more than you have to fit all your code into a single function).

## Chapter 4

XML

Unless you've been living under a rock for the last decade, you'll know that flat text is passé. These days, almost everything is represented using some kind of markup: HTML for web pages and its cousin XML for spreadsheets, web server configuration files, and books like this one. If you're crunching data, the odds are pretty good that your input, your output, or both will use some kind of marked-up format.

Luckily, there's a whole bunch of tools for dealing with marked-up data. After a quick introduction to HTML and XML, this chapter describes DOM and SAX, the two most popular of those tools, which have been implemented in many languages. After that, we take a look at XSLT, a language designed expressly to inspect and transform XML.

One thing we *won't* discuss in this chapter is WYSIWYG tools for editing and transforming XML. Like programmable editors (Section 2.5, *Including One File in Another*, on page 28), these are often the quickest way to solve small problems in isolation, but it's difficult to connect them with other tools to make a data crunching pipeline. They're still handy to have on your desktop, though; two I'd particularly recommend are Altova's XMLSpy,[1] a high-end commercial product, and the XMLBuddy [2] plugin for Eclipse.

4.1 A Quick Introduction

If you've ever written a web page, you probably already know most of what's in this section. Feel free to skip over it or to watch *The Simpsons* with one eye while reading it.

---

[1] http://www.altova.com/products_ide.html
[2] http://xmlbuddy.com

History

In the beginning, there was GML, the Generalized Markup Language, and its successor SGML, the Standard Generalized Markup Language. These were developed between 1969 and 1986 by Charles Goldfarb and others at IBM as a way of adding information to medical and legal documents so that computers could process them. For example, instead of just having a person's name, like Alfred E. Neumann, an SGML document would have:

```
<person role="litigant">Alfred E. Neumann</person>
```

or even:

```
<person role="litigant">
  <given-name>Alfred E.</given-name>
  <surname>Neumann</surname>
</person>
```

so that people could search databases to find cases in which Mr. Neumann had sued, as opposed to ones in which he had been sued.

SGML was a great invention but had one major drawback: its size. By the mid-1980s, the full SGML specification was more than 500 pages long. Writing software that followed all those rules was so daunting that only a few companies ever tried.

In 1989, though, when Tim Berners-Lee needed a way to describe titles, underlining, and cross-references for something he called the World Wide Web, he drew inspiration from SGML. His format, called the HyperText Markup Language, or HTML, had only a small, fixed set of tags. Some of these were semantic, such as "this is a level two heading", while others had a purely visual role, like the ones that *italicized* text. SGML purists sneered at HTML's simplicity, but that simplicity meant that anyone could write it. Within just a few years, millions of people around the world did exactly that.

Almost as soon as HTML appeared, programmers began adding their own extensions to it. This soon led to XML, the eXtensible Markup Language, the first version of which was approved in 1998. XML isn't actually a markup language, like HTML. Instead, it is a set of rules that particular markup languages must obey. While it is much more complex than HTML, it is still simpler than SGML, and has taken the world by storm.

As a result, three kinds of marked-up documents are common:

- Legacy HTML, which doesn't obey XML's rules. For example, web designers who type tags in by hand often don't bother to mark the end of a paragraph; instead, they just start a new one, trusting the browser to know what they mean. This makes automatic processing painful and error-prone. If you have to deal with legacy HTML, the best approach is to convert it to proper XHTML (using Perl's HTML::Tidy module, for example) and use the tools and techniques discussed in this chapter.

- XHTML, which is classic HTML that conforms to XML's rules. Most WYSIWYG editors and software libraries now generate this, but it's worth checking a few samples before you start crunching: much of the XHTML in the world is still typed in by hand, which means that errors are common.

- Everything else. XML-conformant markup is used for everything from images (SVG) to music (MusiXML), chemical formulae (ChemML), and news headlines (RSS). Almost all of this data is created by machines, so it is both more likely to be correctly formatted and more verbose than handwritten HTML or XHTML.

Formatting Rules

An XML document is a tree containing *elements* and *text*. Elements are shown using *tags*; the text is the stuff between the tags.

elements

text

tags

At their simplest, tags are keywords enclosed in angle brackets, like *<this>* and *<that>*. Every opening tag of the form *<example>* must be matched by the corresponding closing tag *</example>*. (Note the slash before the tag name.) Everything between the two is the element's content. If there's no content—in other words, if the closing tag comes immediately after the opening tag, as in *<blah></blah>*—the shorthand notation *<blah/>* (with the slash at the *end* of the tag) can be used.

Since XML documents are trees, elements must be closed in the reverse order that they were opened. This means that <a><b><c></c></b></a> is legal, but <a><b><c></a></b></c> isn't. XML documents must also have a single *root element*; in other words, each document must be a single tree, not a forest.

root element

Let's look at an HTML page for example. Some common, basic tags used in HTML documents include:

<html>	HTML page (must be the document root)
<body>	Body of page (visible content)
<h1>	Level one heading
<h2>, *<h3>*, *<h4>*	Subheading, subsubheading, etc.
<p>	Paragraph
<em>	Emphasized (italics)
<strong>	Emphasized (bold)

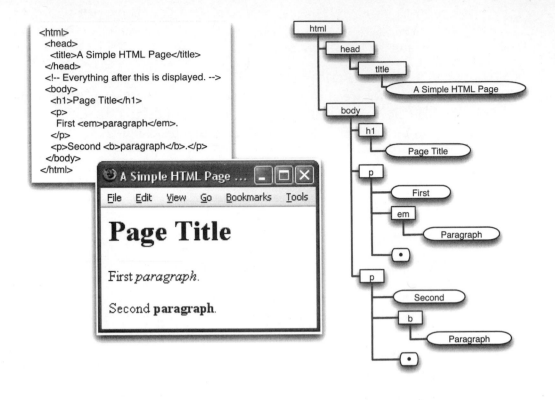

Figure 4.1: HTML DOCUMENT TREE

Now take a look at Figure 4.1 The source to the HTML page, which is stored as a text file, is shown at the upper-left. When this file is handed to Firefox, it translates the content into a tree in memory (shown on the right) and then displays that tree (you can probably guess by now).

Every page has exactly one *<html>* element, which must be the root of the document. This may contain one *<head>* element and *must* contain one *<body>* element. The head stores information like the page's author, version number, and so on; this information isn't displayed but is used by search engines and other tools. The body contains all the text that's to be shown to the user, along with references to images, sound files, and other content discussed in a moment. Finally, everything between <!-- and --> is a comment.

Markup gets more interesting when you start adding attributes to the elements. An *attribute* is just a name/value pair associated with an element. Attributes are written inside the opening tag of an element as name="value". An element may

Joe Asks. . .

When Should I Use Attributes Rather Than Elements?

Strictly speaking, attributes are redundant, since

```
<a b="c">
  <d e="f"/>
</a>
```

could always be written as

```
<a>
  <a-b>c</a-b>
  <d><d-e>f</d-e></d>
</a>
```

Attributes are a lot easier for people to type in, though, so the question arises: when should you use attributes *vs.* nested elements?

The answer is that you should use attributes only when

- each value can occur at most once for any element,
- the order of the values doesn't matter,
- those values have no internal structure, and
- the values themselves are short.

The first two rules come from XML's insistence that any attribute appear only once for a given tag and that attributes can't contain elements. The third is mostly a question of readability: if you try to put too much data in an attribute, it becomes impossible to see the document's structure.

have any number of attributes, but any attribute can be used only once with any particular element. Every attribute must have a value, and every value must be quoted. (Most browsers still accept legacy HTML such as *<tag color=blue>* and *<tag invisible>*, but neither is strictly legal: the first because the value isn't quoted, the second because the value is missing entirely.)

If you want to put a quotation mark inside an attribute value, or an angle bracket in text, you have to escape it. Escape sequences start with & and end with ;. In between, you can put the character's numeric code, as in *£* (which should display £). Alternatively, if the character you want is commonly used, it may have a descriptive name. The most common are *<, >, &,* and *",* for <, >, &, and " respectively. You can find a complete list online.[3]

---

[3]http://www.w3.org/TR/REC-html40/sgml/entities.html

Links

HTML really earns its H when you start adding links between pages. Links are specified using the <a> element with an href= attribute, whose value specifies what the link points at. The text inside the element gives the viewer something to click on to follow the link. For example, the link

```
<a href="http://www.pragprog.com">Pragmatic!</a>
```

is displayed as—oh, you know how links work.

Confusingly, <a> can also be used to create an *anchor* inside a document. An anchor is just a point in the document that some other document can point to. To specify an anchor, use an <a> element with a name= attribute instead of an href= attribute. The name= attribute's value can be pretty much any string you want, although almost everyone uses descriptive labels like *first_citation* or *chapter:testing*. Another document can then point to that anchor by specifying its name after a # in an href=, as in *http://com.com/index.html#mid*.

4.2 SAX

SAX, the Simple API for XML, turns an XML document into a stream of events; users then write code to handle those events. This "inside out" model will be familiar to anyone who has done any GUI programming: instead of writing an entire program top-down, you hand control over to a framework, which calls your code when it needs to do so.

Like everything else, SAX has strengths and weaknesses. Its main strengths are that simple things are simple to write and that it can handle very large documents, since it stores only a small fragment of the document in memory at any time.

That feature is also SAX's greatest weakness. If you want to modify the document's structure, or if you need a broader context in order to decide what to do at some point, you have to keep track of where you are manually. It's rather like sorting or reversing the lines in a file when all you have is a method to read one line at a time: you have to create the necessary data structures yourself.

Getting Started

Python's implementation of SAX lives in the xml.sax module. This module contains a method called parse(), which does what its name suggests: parses an XML document. It takes an object as an argument; each time it encounters something interesting, like a tag or a piece of text, it calls one of that object's methods. (Java's org.xml.sax and Perl's XML::Parser::PerlSax work in more or less the same way.)

The object you pass to parse() must be derived from a class called ContentHandler, which is also in the xml.sax module. By default, ContentHandler's methods do nothing; in order to actually process the XML that's being parsed, you have to override one or more of the methods that handle

- the start and end of the entire document,

- the start and end of individual elements,

- text, and

- ignorable whitespace (which we will ignore for now).

If you've ever done any GUI programming, this should seem eerily familiar. Overriding a method to handle an opening tag event is exactly like overriding the method on a button that handles mouse-down or the method on a text widget that handles character insertion. In each case, the framework (SAX, or your GUI toolkit) takes care of the routine stuff. All you provide is the little bit of logic that's specific to your application.

Let's look at an example. Suppose we want to print out all the opening tags in an XML document. The first step is to derive a class, which we'll call ShowTags, and override its startElement() method. This method takes two parameters: the name of the element and a dictionary of its attributes. We then create an instance of this class, and pass it to parse(), along with the stream the parser is to read. The whole thing is as simple as

```python
import sys
from xml.sax import parse, ContentHandler

class ShowTags(ContentHandler):
    def startElement(self, name, attrs):
        print name

handler = ShowTags()
parse(sys.stdin, handler)
```

If we hand this little program the following document

```
<html>
<head>
<title>A Simple Document</title>
<meta name="author" content="Greg Wilson"/>
</head>
<body>
<h1>A Simple Document</h1>
<p>This document shows how SAX (the
    <b>S</b>imple <b>A</b>PI for <b>X</b>ML)
    works.
</p>
<hr/> <!-- put a line between paragraphs -->
<p align="center">And that's all.</p>
</body>
</html>
```

it prints

```
html
head
title
meta
body
h1
p
b
b
b
hr
p
```

Let's make the output a little more readable by indenting tags to show how elements are nested. To do this, we need to count how many opening and closing tags we've seen. The IndentTags class shown below does this by overriding endElement() as well as startElement():

```python
import sys
from xml.sax import parse, ContentHandler

class IndentTags(ContentHandler):
    def __init__(self):
        self.indent = 0
    def startElement(self, name, attrs):
        print ' ' * self.indent + name
        self.indent += 1
    def endElement(self, name):
        self.indent -= 1
handler = IndentTags()
parse(sys.stdin, handler)
```

Its output for the same document is

```
html
 head
  title
  meta
 body
  h1
  p
   b
   b
   b
  hr
  p
```

Example: Creating an Attribute Inventory

You have lots of ways to specify how the elements in an XML document can be nested and what attributes they're allowed to have (see the sidebar on page 89). In practice, though, you often have nothing to work with except the document itself. In these cases, you often have to reverse engineer the document's format before you can start crunching it.

One piece of information you might find useful when you're doing this is an inventory of which attributes are used with each element. For example, in the simple document shown earlier, the *<meta>* element had name= and content= attributes, while the *<p>* element had an align= attribute.

Building an attribute inventory is simple, as SAX hands the startElement() method a dictionary holding the names and values of the element's attributes. To keep track of them, let's give our content handler class a dictionary as a member. Its keys are the names of the elements we've seen so far; each value is a list of the attribute names associated with that element. The program is

```python
import sys
from xml.sax import parse, ContentHandler

class ShowAttr(ContentHandler):

    def __init__(self):
        self.table = {}

    def startElement(self, name, attrs):
        if name in self.table:
            seen = self.table[name]
        else:
            seen = []
        for a in attrs.keys():
            if a not in seen:
                seen.append(a)
        self.table[name] = seen

handler = ShowAttr()
parse(sys.stdin, handler)
elements = handler.table.keys()
elements.sort()
for e in elements:
    attrs = handler.table[e]
    if attrs:
        attrs.sort()
        print e, ":", ', '.join(attrs)
    else:
        print e
```

and it produces

```
b
body
h1
head
hr
html
meta : content, name
p : align
title
```

Handling Errors

Now, what happens when things go wrong? In particular, what happens if the tags in the XML document aren't properly nested or if someone doesn't put quotes around an attribute value? By default, Python (and Java) print a stack trace, but it would be nice to get something that tells us where in the document the error occurred, so that we can fix it.

You customize SAX's error handling by deriving a class from xml.sax.ErrorHandler. Its three methods fatalError(), error(), and warning() each take an exception as an argument. This exception's getLineNumber() and getColNumber() methods specify where the error was detected; its getMessage() method specifies the error.

Installing a custom error handler is as simple as passing an instance of your class as the third argument of parse(). For example, a simple program that I use to check that the chapters of this book are properly formatted is

```python
import sys
from xml.sax import ContentHandler, parse, ErrorHandler

class ReportError(ErrorHandler):
    def fatalError(self, exception):
        self.printError("FATAL", exception)
    def error(self, exception):
        self.printError("ERROR", exception)
    def warning(self, exception):
        self.printError("WARNING", exception)
    def printError(self, level, exc):
        line = exc.getLineNumber()
        column = exc.getColumnNumber()
        loc = "(%d, %d)" % (line, column)
        msg = exc.getMessage()
        print "%s%s: %s" % (level, loc, msg)

if __name__ == "__main__":
    xmlHandler = ContentHandler()
    errHandler = ReportError()
    parse(sys.stdin, xmlHandler, errHandler)
```

(If you're new to Python, the line

```python
if __name__ == "__main__":
```

just means, "if this program is being run directly from the command line." If the program is being imported into another program, the lines below this one won't be executed.)

While this is better than a stack trace, it's still not good enough. The most common error in handwritten XML is forgetting to close a tag, but ReportError() can't tell us which tag we forgot to close, since it doesn't save state. All it knows is that it found </x> when it was expecting </y>.

The solution is to keep a stack of open tags while parsing and print that stack when a mismatch is found. The following Checker class does this. Note that it is derived from both ContentHandler and ErrorHandler, so it handles errors as well as normal processing events. This makes code easier to manage, but we have to remember to pass a single instance of the class to parse() twice (once for handling content and once for handling errors).

Negative Indexing

One of the little things I like most about Python is the way it handles indexing. If you have a list *Q*, then *Q[0]* is the first element, *Q[1]* the second, and so on, just as in most other languages. In Python, though, *Q[-1]* isn't an error: it's the *last* element in the list, and *Q[-2]* is the second to last. No more typing *Q[len(Q)-1]* to peel the tail off a queue....

Python also lets you take a *slice* out of a list. If you want items 2, 3, and 4, for example, you type *Q[2:5]*. Slices include their lower bound, but not their upper, so *Q[0:len(Q)]* works like

```
for (i=0; i<len(Q); i++) {
    ...stuff...
}
```

in C or Java. Put the two together, and *Q[0:-1]* means, "Everything in the list except the last element."

```python
import sys
from xml.sax import ContentHandler, parse, ErrorHandler

class Checker(ContentHandler, ErrorHandler):

    # Construct a checker.
    def __init__(self):
        ContentHandler.__init__(self)
        self.stack = []

    # When an opening tag is seen, push its name on the stack.
    def startElement(self, name, attrs):
        self.stack.append(name)

    # When a closing tag is seen, check it, then pop the stack.
    def endElement(self, name):
        assert name == self.stack[-1]
        self.stack = self.stack[0:-1]

    # Handle exceptions during processing.
    def handleExc(self, exc):
        line = exc.getLineNumber()
        column = exc.getColumnNumber()
        msg = exc.getMessage()
        print "%s (%d %d)" % (msg, line, column)
        for tag in self.stack:
            print tag
        sys.exit(1)

    # Redirect warnings, errors, and fatal errors to handleExc.
    warning = handleExc
    error = handleExc
    fatalError = handleExc

# Run the program from the command line.
if __name__ == "__main__":
    handler = Checker()
    parse(sys.stdin, handler, handler)
```

Running this program on the following badly formatted document:

```
Line 1   <html>
   -     <head>
   -     <title>A Simple Document</title>
   -     <meta name="author" content="Greg Wilson"/>
   5     </head>
   -     <body>
   -     <h1>A Simple Document
   -     <p>This document shows how SAX (the
   -        <b>S</b>imple <b>A</b>PI for <b>X</b>ML)
  10        works.
   -     </h1></p>
   -     <hr/> <!-- put a line between paragraphs -->
   -     <p align="center">And that's all.</p>
   -     </body>
  15     </html>
```

produces

```
mismatched tag (11 2)
html
body
h1
p
```

Example: Normalizing a Document

Now let's try something more ambitious. Suppose we want to normalize a document by converting every *<tag></tag>* pair into *<tag/>*. We can't do this inside any single method call since we don't know what to print for an opening tag until we see what comes after it.

write-behind

The solution is to use a strategy called *write-behind*, in which we're always writing data a little behind what we're reading. When we see the start of an element, we don't print it right away.

Instead, we save everything we need to know about the opening tag and wait for the next event. If it's the matching end tag, we print the shorthand form. If it's

DTDs, Schemas, and All That

You have several ways to define how elements in an XML document can be nested, what attributes they may have, and what kinds of values they can contain. The oldest, and still most widely used, is the Document Type Definition, or *DTD*. DTDs use a syntax reminiscent of regular expressions to specify nesting and allowed attributes, but don't allow developers to restrict the kinds of values elements can contain (e.g., numerical, dates, and so on).

The W3C's XML Schema specification, available at `http://www.w3.org/XML/Schema`, remedies this shortcoming, and is itself defined in XML, but XML Schema definitions can quickly become mind-numbingly verbose. RELAX NG (`http://www.relaxng.org`) is simpler, both to read and to write, but isn't (yet) as widely supported. (Har03) contains a good discussion of the strengths and weaknesses of these and others.

anything else, such as text or the start of another element, we print a standard opening tag.

Before starting our implementation, we have to decide what to do about attributes. SAX passes attributes to our startElement() method in a dictionary. This means that we have no way to know the order in which those attributes appeared in the original document. For example, we would get the dictionary

```
{"a" : "able", "b" : "baker", "c" : "charlie"}
```

for any of the following six opening tags:

```
<tag a="able"    b="baker"   c="charlie"/>
<tag a="able"    c="charlie" b="baker"/>
<tag b="baker"   a="able"    c="charlie"/>
<tag b="baker"   c="charlie" a="able"/>
<tag c="charlie" a="able"    b="baker"/>
<tag c="charlie" b="baker"   a="able"/>
```

We also can't reproduce the whitespace inside the element (that is, the spaces between the elements inside each tag), since SAX doesn't record it anywhere.

Is this a problem? That depends what you're trying to do. Elliotte Rusty Harold and other XML gurus believe that 99.9% of the time, if you're worrying about attribute order and preserving comments, you're thinking at the wrong level.[4] In

---

[4]See `http://www.cafeconleche.org/books/effectivexml/chapters/15.html`

the other 0.1% of cases—writing a WYSIWYG XML editor, for example—the only solution is to write your own specialized XML parser.

Back to our normalizer...When SAX calls our startElement() method, we flush any pending output and convert the tag name and attribute dictionary to an almost-complete opening tag. If the next thing we see is text, ignorable whitespace, or another opening tag, we print the pending opening tag as normal. If the next thing we see is a closing tag, though, we print the opening tag in shorthand form.

Note that we don't have to check whether the closing tag name matches the opening tag name: if there's anything between the opening and closing tag, some other method will be called before endElement(), and that method will take care of flushing the pending output.

```python
import sys
from xml.sax import ContentHandler, parse, ErrorHandler

class Normalizer(ContentHandler):

    # Construct a normalizer.
    def __init__(self, stream):
        self.stream = stream
        self.pending = None

    # Record the details of an opening tag.
    def startElement(self, name, attrs):
        self.makePending(name, attrs)

    # Handle a closing tag by closing the short form opening tag,
    # or by writing out the closing tag on its own.
    def endElement(self, name):
        if self.pending:
            self.stream.write(self.pending + "/>")
        else:
            self.stream.write("</" + name + ">")
        self.pending = None

    # On text and ignorable whitespace, write any pending opening
    # tags using the normal form.
    def characters(self, text):
        self.clearPending(text)

    def ignorableWhitespace(self, text):
        self.clearPending(text)

    # Record enough about an opening tag to reproduce it.
    def makePending(self, name, attrs):
        self.clearPending()
        self.pending = "<" + name
        keys = attrs.keys()
        keys.sort()
        for k in keys:
            self.pending += ' %s="%s"' % (k, attrs[k])

    # Clear the pending opening tag if intervening text is seen.
    def clearPending(self, text=""):
        if self.pending:
            self.stream.write(self.pending + ">")
            self.pending = None
        self.stream.write(text)
```

```
# Run the program from the command line.
if __name__ == "__main__":
    handler = Normalizer(sys.stdout)
    parse(sys.stdin, handler, handler)
```

Just to check that it works, let's feed it this file:

```
<html>
<body>
<h1 align="center">Heading</h1>
<hr></hr>
<p highlight="no" class="opening">Paragraph.</p>
<p></p> <!-- empty -->
<p> </p> <!-- not empty -->
<p><em>Something</em> inside a paragraph <b></b>.</p>
</body>
</html>
```

The output is

```
<html>
<body>
<h1 align="center">Heading</h1>
<hr/>
<p class="opening" highlight="no">Paragraph.</p>
<p/>
<p> </p>
<p><em>Something</em> inside a paragraph <b/>.</p>
</body>
</html>
```

As predicted, the order of the first paragraph's attributes has changed. We've also lost the comments, since SAX doesn't report them to our event handler.

Limitations

SAX's greatest strength is its simplicity, but that very simplicity makes it unsuitable for tricky problems. Suppose, for example, that we have 1100 documents, half of which put links outside headings like this:

```
<a href="http://www.pragprog.com"><h1>Be Pragmatic</h1></a>
```

and the rest of which put them inside, like this:

```
<h1><a href="http://www.pragprog.com">Be Pragmatic</a></h1>
```

In order to simplify other kinds of processing, we'd like to normalize these so that the anchors always appear outside the headings.

How would we do this with SAX? Following on from the previous example, it looks like we should record every heading tag we see (<h1> through <h4>) and then check whether the tag immediately after it is an anchor. If it is, we print them in reverse order; if it isn't, we print both whatever is pending and what we've just seen.

That sounds a little trickier than I'd like, but still doable. In the real world, though, we may need to do things that are a *lot* trickier, and that's where SAX comes up short. Suppose, for exampe, that we're trying to reformat some tables that were produced by one vendor's spreadsheet so that we can use them with another's. The first spreadsheet saves the tables like this:

```
<table columns="L(Year)L(Month)R($)">
  <row>
    <col>2004</col>
    <col>Dec</col>
    <col>2740.23</col>
  </row>
  <row>
    <col>2005</col>
    <col>Jan</col>
    <col>3137.99</col>
  </row>
</table>
```

while the second spreadsheet wants

```
<table columns="3">
  <titlerow>
    <titlecol align="left" title="Year"/>
    <titlecol align="left" title="Month"/>
    <titlecol align="right" title="$"/>
  </titlerow>
  <row>
    <col align="left">2004</col>
    <col align="left">Dec</col>
    <col align="right">2740.23</col>
  </row>
  <row>
    <col align="left">2005</col>
    <col align="left">Jan</col>
    <col align="right">3137.99</col>
  </row>
</table>
```

Generating the title row and title columns won't be too bad: we can parse the input table's columns attribute and then immediately print the <*titlerow*> element. But what about the columns in the table itself? In order to get the right values for their align= attributes, we'll have to keep track of whether we're in the first, second, or third column every time we see a <*td*> element. It's doable, but it's a pain to code and debug, and Turing help us if tables are ever nested.

The point of this example is that SAX has limits. When you're crunching data, you'll run into them pretty quickly: on even moderately complicated problems, you'll quickly find that you're building complicated data structures in memory in order to keep track of where exactly you are in the XML. Rather than doing this, you should move on to our second tool for manipulating XML: the Document Object Model.

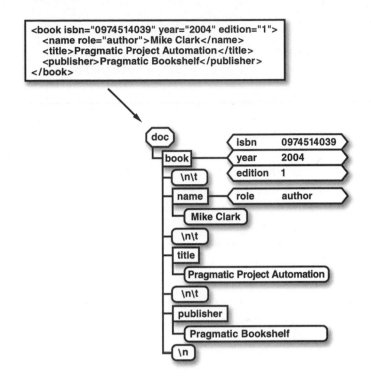

Figure 4.2: A DOM Tree

4.3 DOM

The Document Object Model, or DOM, is a cross-language API that treats XML as a tree, rather than as a stream. DOM makes it much easier to manipulate the document's structure but may require a lot of memory for large documents.

The official specification for DOM comes from the World Wide Web Consortium (W3C). Unfortunately, its "lowest common denominator" approach means that every language's API looks more or less like C. Other implementations, like Java's JDOM (http://www.jdom.org) and Python's xml.dom.minidom, fit their languages much better and are more widely used. An example is shown in Figure 4.2.

One thing to keep clear is that DOM is *not* a parser. In order to build a DOM tree in memory, an application must provide a parser itself. As you might guess, DOM trees are often built using SAX.

Getting Started

DOM trees follow a few simple rules. First, every document has a document node at its root. This has a single child, which is the document's root element. The root element's children can be other element nodes, text nodes, or other things such as processing instructions and entity definitions that we won't worry about for now. It's important to note that DOM creates nodes for whitespace, such as the end-of-line carriage returns. One of the most common mistakes beginners make is to forget about these.

The two main classes in this structure are Document and Node. In Python's minidom, Document has a member called documentElement, which is (unsurprisingly) the root element of the document. Node has a member called parentNode, which refers to the node's parent, and two concrete subclasses: Element and Text. Element's two main members are tagName and childNodes; Text's main member is data, which is the text that the node includes. Here's our first DOM program:

```python
import sys
from xml.dom.minidom import parse

doc = parse(sys.stdin)
root = doc.documentElement
for child in root.childNodes:
    if child.nodeType is doc.ELEMENT_NODE:
        print child.tagName
```

As you can probably guess from reading it, this program parses an XML document and then prints out the tags of its top-level elements. When fed an HTML page, for example, it prints out

```
head
body
```

We can do the same thing in Java using the JDOM library:

```java
import java.util.Iterator;
import org.jdom.Document;
import org.jdom.Element;
import org.jdom.input.SAXBuilder;
class ShowTop {
    public static void main(String[] args) {
        try {
            SAXBuilder builder = new SAXBuilder();
            Document doc = builder.build(args[0]);

            Element root = doc.getRootElement();
            Iterator ic = root.getChildren().iterator();
            while (ic.hasNext()) {
                Element elt = (Element)ic.next();
                System.out.println(elt.getName());
            }
        } catch (Exception e) {
            System.err.println(e);
        }
    }
}
```

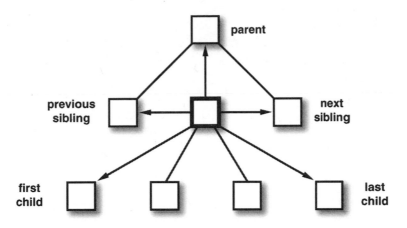

parent

previous sibling

next sibling

first child

last child

Figure 4.3: RELATIONSHIPS AMONG DOM TREE NODES

Either way, it's pretty boring. How about printing out all the tags, indented to show structure?

```
import sys
from xml.dom.minidom import parse

def show(node, indent=0):
    if node.nodeType is node.ELEMENT_NODE:
        print (indent * ' ') + node.tagName
        for child in node.childNodes:
            show(child, indent+1)
doc = parse(sys.stdin)
show(doc.documentElement)
```

Pretty simple, isn't it? It's sometimes easy to forget, amid the hype, that XML is really just a way to describe trees.

The minidom library includes a few other functions that I use all the time. By far the most useful is getElementsByTagName(), which finds all the elements below a particular node that have the specified tag name. Nodes also have helper methods to get at nearby elements in the tree (Figure 4.3):

- firstChild() and lastChild() get a node's first and last child nodes.
- previousSibling() and nextSibling() get the nodes before and after a particular node in the tree.

All of these methods return None if the node in question doesn't exist.

Using these methods, you can extract all the acronyms in a document:

```
Line 1    import sys
    -     from xml.dom.minidom import parse
    -
    -     doc = parse(sys.stdin)
    5     nodes = doc.getElementsByTagName("acronym")
    -     for node in nodes:
    -         print node.firstChild.data
```

Given the input

```
<html>
<body>
<ul>
  <li><acronym>TLA</acronym>: Three Letter Acronym.</li>
  <li><acronym>XTLA</acronym>: Extended Three Letter Acronym.</li>
  <li><acronym>YAMA</acronym>: Yet Another Meaningless Acronym.</li>
</ul>
</body>
</html>
```

this program prints

```
TLA
XTLA
YAMA
```

Note the use of firstChild() on line 7. The program needs to use this because the text data isn't stored directly under the <acronym> tag. Instead, it's stored inside a text node that is the <acronym>'s only child.

As simple as it is, this little program is the backbone of most of the XML crunching I do. It reads in the document I'm processing, finds the elements I care about, and pulls some data out of them. Larger versions might loop over several documents, or search for specific elements below the ones found by the outermost getElementsByTagName(), but the basic design is always the same.

Let's keep going. Suppose we want to strip all the markup out of an HTML page in order to feed the page through a spell-checking program. Here's a simple Python program that does what we want:

```
import sys
from xml.dom.minidom import parse
def concatText(node):
    result = ""
    if node.nodeType is node.TEXT_NODE:
        result = node.data
    elif node.nodeType is node.ELEMENT_NODE:
        for child in node.childNodes:
            result += concatText(child)
    return result
root = parse(sys.stdin).documentElement
print concatText(root)
```

The recursive function concatText() does all the work. If the node is a text node, we just return its data (line 6); if it's an element, we concatenate the text of all the nodes below it and return that (line 8).

This is pretty inefficient, since we'll be concatenating lots of little strings, then concatenating the results to create larger ones, and so on. If we care about performance, we can speed this up by putting all the text in a list and concatenating it all in one go at the end:

```
import sys
from xml.dom.minidom import parse

def concatText(node, result=None):
    if result is None:
        temp = []
    else:
        temp = result
    if node.nodeType is node.TEXT_NODE:
        temp.append(node.data)
    elif node.nodeType is node.ELEMENT_NODE:
        for child in node.childNodes:
            concatText(child, temp)
    if result is None:
        return ''.join(temp)
    else:
        return None
root = parse(sys.stdin).documentElement
print concatText(root)
```

Attributes

The last core feature of DOM is how it represents attributes. As you might expect after seeing SAX, DOM element nodes have an attributes member, which is a dictionary[5] whose keys are attribute names. Just to keep things confusing, the values in attributes aren't actually the attribute values; instead, each is an instance of a class called Attr, whose value member is the actual value.

We can use this to build yet another attribute concordance generator:

```
import sys
from xml.dom.minidom import parse

def concordance(node, result):
    seen = result.get(node.tagName, [])
    attrs = node.attributes
    for key in attrs.keys():
        if key not in seen:
            seen.append(key)
    result[node.tagName] = seen
    for child in node.childNodes:
        if child.nodeType is child.ELEMENT_NODE:
            concordance(child, result)
    return result
doc = parse(sys.stdin)
c = concordance(doc.documentElement, {})
for key in c:
    print key, ' '.join(c[key])
```

---

[5]Actually, it's an instance of a class that implements most of same methods as a dictionary.

Inserting Content

I said at the start of this section that DOM made it easier to manipulate the structure of XML. To prove this, let's take a look at how we would number the paragraphs in a document. Mutating the text node under the <p> node doesn't work because the paragraph might look like this:

```
<p><em>Accentuate</em> the positive.</p>
```

The right solution is to create a new text node and insert it in front of the <p> node's existing children. You'd think that creating a new node would be as simple as calling the appropriate class's constructor, but DOM likes to keep track of which documents nodes belong to, so instead of providing constructors, it uses the document object as a *factory* for creating nodes. Document's createElement() and createTextNode() do the obvious: the first takes a tag name as its sole argument, the second takes a string representing the content of the text node.

Once nodes have been created, adding them to the tree is easy. Every node has a method called insertBefore(new, old), which puts the new node just in front of an existing child. If you want to put the new node at the end of the child list, appendChild(new) does the trick. Let's number some paragraphs:

```python
import sys
from xml.dom.minidom import parse

doc = parse(sys.stdin)
paras = doc.getElementsByTagName("p")
count = 0
for para in paras:
    count += 1
    str = "(%d) " % count
    newNode = doc.createTextNode(str)
    para.insertBefore(newNode, para.firstChild)
    para.normalize()
print doc.toxml()
```

Instead of recursing, we use getElementsByTagName() to find all the paragraphs. We then create and insert a text node showing the paragraph number and call normalize(), which will collapse the contiguous text nodes into one. (This isn't strictly necessary, but if the text was normalized before, we might as well leave it normalized afterward.) Finally, we convert the document we've modified back to a string for printing. It comes out as

```xml
<?xml version="1.0" ?>
<html>
<body>
<p>(1) The first paragraph.</p>
<p>(2) <em>The</em> second.</p>
<h3>A heading</h3>
<p>(3) <em>Another</em> paragraph.</p>
</body>
</html>
```

Note that doc.toxml() has put an XML version header at the start of the document. Strictly speaking, all of our documents should include one of these—even HTML pages—but like most people, we're lazy.

Deleting Content

Finally, let's take a look at how to remove nodes from the tree entirely. We have to be a little careful about doing this because Python and Java are garbage-collected languages. If we delete the last reference to something, the garbage collector could decide that's a good time to recycle the memory for it and its children.

The solution? Remove the node we want to get rid of from the tree, but *keep a reference to it* and delete it only after we've moved its children somewhere safe. For example:

```
import sys
from xml.dom.minidom import parse

doc = parse(sys.stdin)
emphs = doc.getElementsByTagName("em")
for node in emphs:
    parent = node.parentNode
    for child in node.childNodes:
        node.removeChild(child)
        parent.insertBefore(child, node)
    parent.removeChild(node)
print doc.toxml()
```

This moves all of the emphasis node's children to just before it in the parent's child list and removes the emphasis node itself only once all its children are relocated (Figure 4.4 on the next page).

Hmm...Does this actually work? Suppose the input contains nested emphasis, like this:

```
<html>
<body>
<p><em>Another <em>emphasized</em></em> paragraph.</p>
</body>
</html>
```

The program shown above prints this:

```
<?xml version="1.0" ?>
<html>
<body>
<p>Another  paragraph.</p>
</body>
</html>
```

The word *emphasized* has disappeared. What happened? Well, it turns out that a node's children are stored in a list-like structure; when a node is removed, all the nodes to its right are bumped down to the left, as shown in Figure 4.5 on page 101.

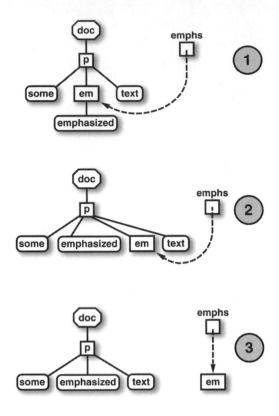

Figure 4.4: REMOVING A NODE

When the text node containing the word *emphasized* was moved up, it was moved up into the upper *<em>* and then thrown away along with it by mistake.

We can avoid this problem using the double-pointer iteration trick familiar to anyone who has ever written a linked list. In the loop over the children of the node we're about to remove, we keep a pointer to both the current node and the next one, assigning the latter to the former on each pass through the loop:

```
import sys
from xml.dom.minidom import parse

doc = parse(sys.stdin)
emphs = doc.getElementsByTagName("em")
for node in emphs:
    parent = node.parentNode
    child = node.firstChild
    while child:
```

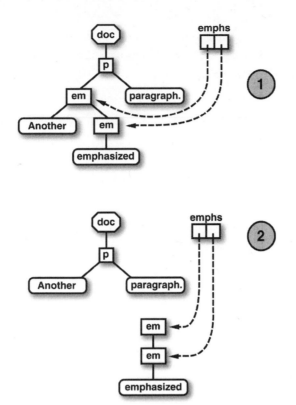

Figure 4.5: REMOVING A NODE—THE PROBLEM

```
        next = child.nextSibling
        node.removeChild(child)
        parent.insertBefore(child, node)
        child = next
    parent.removeChild(node)
print doc.toxml()
```

This time the output is correct:

```
<?xml version="1.0" ?>
<html>
<body>
<p>Another emphasized paragraph.</p>
</body>
</html>
```

4.4 XPath

Good programmers solve problems. Great ones build tools that make it trivial to solve entire classes of problems. Unfortunately, the most widely used tool custom-built to work with XML, called XSL, is only almost great.

XSL has three parts. The first is XPath, a W3C standard for specifying sets of nodes in an XML document. The second, XSLT, provides a way to translate one XML format to another, or from XML to HTML, PDF, plain text, and just about anything else. Finally, XSL-FO (the FO stands for "formatting objects") allows you to typeset output and is outside the scope of this book.

Let's start with XPath, which defines a way to specify nodes in an XML document that looks a lot like the notation we all use to identify files and directories. For example, suppose we have the files and folders shown in Figure 4.6 on the next page. The expression /home/gvwilson identifies my home directory, while /dev/audio/mx01 is the audio mixer attached to my computer. These are both *absolute paths*; in other words, they refer to the same things no matter where you are. An expression like bin/oonix, on the other hand, is a *relative path*: if your current working directory is /home/gvwilson, it points at one thing, while if you're in /home/dave, it points at another.

So, consider this XML document, which records issues in a trouble ticket system:

```
<?xml version="1.0" encoding="ISO-8859-1"?>
<project>
  <ticket id="1720" status="open" priority="2">
    <author>Dave Thomas</author>
    <comment>
      <author>Andy Hunt</author>
      Bah!
    </comment>
  </ticket>
  <ticket id="1774" status="rejected" priority="5">
    <author>Dave Thomas</author>
  </ticket>
  <ticket id="1803" status="open" priority="4">
    <author>Greg Wilson</author>
    <comment>
      <author>Andy Hunt</author>
      OK, this one I believe.
    </comment>
  </ticket>
</project>
```

The XPath expression */project* is an absolute path that specifies exactly one node: the root element of the document. The expression */project/ticket* is also an absolute path but specifies the set of all <*ticket*> elements that are directly below the root <*project*> element. Unlike paths in a file system, an XPath expression can produce a set of values, rather than just one.

Figure 4.6: SAMPLE FILES AND FOLDERS

Finally, the expression */project/ticket/author* selects all of the *<author>* elements in tickets. It doesn't select the authors of the comments contained inside those tickets; you'd need to use */project/ticket/comment/author* to get them.

Relative paths work exactly as you'd expect. If your current node is the root *project* node, the expression *ticket* selects all the tickets immediately below it. The expression *author* selects nothing below the root *project* element, but if evaluated for a particular ticket, it selects just that ticket's author, and so on.

The fact that a path identifies a set of nodes, rather than a single node, is one of the big differences between XPath and your file system. Another is that XPath provides a richer set of ways to specify paths. If a path starts with a double slash //, for example, then *all* the elements in the document that match will be returned.[6] This means that //*author* will return both the authors of tickets and the authors of comments.

As with file systems, the wildcard * can be used to match unknown elements in paths. Each * matches one path element, so /*project*/*/*author* matches all the *author* grandchildren of the root *project* node. In the previous example document, the resulting set of nodes includes both the authors of tickets and the authors of comments. This can be combined with the double slash to create //*, which selects all the document's elements.

Predicates

But suppose you want only tickets that are still open? You could get a node set back from XPath, and then iterate through it, selecting nodes with *status="open"* in their attributes. Alternatively, you could add a *predicate* to the expression to narrow the set of nodes you want XPath to return. Predicates are enclosed in square brackets; to refer to an attribute value, put @ in front of the attribute's name, and specify the value you want it to have. So /*project*/*ticket[@status='open']* will get open tickets, while /*project*/*ticket[@status='open']*/*author* will get all the authors of open tickets.

Predicates can also be used with numeric values. /*project*/*ticket[@priority>3]*, for example, selects only high-priority tickets, while *[@priority>3 and @status='open']* gets tickets that are both high priorities, and still open. It's a lot easier than writing the equivalent SAX or DOM code....

Why is the @ sign needed? Because if you don't include it, XPath evaluates the predicate using child elements, rather than attributes. The predicate expression //*author[note]* selects only those <*author*> elements that have a <*note*> element as an immediate child (remember, // searches the entire document), while //*author[title='Dr']* selects only those authors having a <*title*> child whose text value is *Dr*.

You can also provide array-style indices as predicates to select children by location. /*project*/*[1]* selects the first child of the project,[7] while /*project*/*[33]* returns the thirty-third if it exists, or an empty list if it doesn't.

Advanced Features

What if you want the last child of an element, rather than the first? Sadly, you can't use negative indices to count backward, as you do in Python: the expression

---

[6]Just as ** means "this directory and all subdirectories" to tools like Ant and some modern shells.
[7]Unlike pretty much everything else designed in the last twenty years, XPath uses one-based counting.

comment

    All comment children of the current node

/comment

    All comment children of the root node

text()

    All text children of the current node

@status

    All status attributes of the current node

*/comment(1)

    The first comment on each node below the current node

../@status

    The status attribute of this node's parent

/project/ticket(2)/comment(last())

    The most recent comment on the second ticket in the project

//ticket(priority>3 and status='open')/comment

    All comments on all open, high-priority tickets

Figure 4.7: XPATH EXPRESSIONS

/project/[-1] doesn't give you what you want. The expression */project/[last()]* does, though, and is a nice segue into the subject of functions.

XPath defines several other functions. The one you'll probably use most often is text(), which returns the text nodes below a particular node. If you actually want to get the comments people have made on open tickets, for example, you would use *//ticket/comment//text().* concat() and starts-with() work on strings; sum() adds up numbers, and so on. The official specification[8] of what functions exist and how they behave is on the web, as well as a shorter version.[9]

One thing XPath *doesn't* give you is a way to define functions of your own. This is a reminder that you shouldn't think of XPath as a full-blown programming language. Instead, like regular expressions, XPath is a way to match patterns and extract information for processing using something else.

The last feature of XPath we'll mention before putting it through its paces is the notion of an *axis*. An axis just defines a set of nodes relative to the current location in the document. So far, we've been using the implicit axis *child* in all of our expressions, since XPath assumes that's what we want unless we tell it to use something else. Many other axes also exist, though, with names like *ancestor-*

---

[8]http://www.w3.org/TR/xpath-functions
[9]http://www.w3schools.com/xpath/xpath_functions.asp

or-self and *following-sibling*. All of the axes XPath supports are described on the web,[10] as well as a diagram showing how they relate to one another.[11] Using axes, we can write expressions like */descendant::author[1]*, which finds the first *<author>* element located anywhere in the document, or an expression such as *//comment/preceding-sibling::author*, which

- finds all *<comment>* elements;
- gets their preceding siblings (i.e., the elements immediately before them that are children of the same parent); and
- selects those that are *<author>* elements.

The rules for evaluating these expressions are well defined, but unless you're working with them every day, you will probably find them confusing to read and write. In practice, I stick to what I can do with the familiar short forms shown in Figure 4.7 on the preceding page.

Using XPath in Programs

XPath may have been designed to be used as part of XSLT, but a lot of programmers find it's very useful on its own. If you're using Python, Fourthought Inc.'s 4Suite (http://4suite.org) is an excellent open source implementation. In Java, I prefer Jaxen (http://jaxen.org), which works both with the official W3C implementation of DOM and with JDOM. Here's a Java program that reads an XML document, applies an XPath expression to it, and prints the results:

```
public class XPath {
    public static void main(String[] args) {
        try {
            SAXBuilder builder = new SAXBuilder();
            Document doc = builder.build(args[0]);
            JDOMXPath x = new JDOMXPath(args[1]);
            List matches = x.selectNodes(doc);

            XMLOutputter fmt = new XMLOutputter();
            int count = 0;
            for (Iterator i = matches.iterator(); i.hasNext(); ) {
                Element e = (Element)i.next();
                System.out.println(count++);
                System.out.println(fmt.outputString(e));
                System.out.println();
            }
        } catch (Exception e) {
            System.err.println(e);
        }
    }
}
```

This code creates a SAXBuilder to parse our XML and then uses it to create a DOM Document out of the file named in the first command-line argument. The second

---

[10]http://www.w3schools.com/xpath/xpath_location.asp
[11]http://nwalsh.com/docs/tutorials/xsl/xsl/foil22.html

command-line argument is the XPath expression we're interested in; we use it to create a JDOMXPath object called *x*, and then call *x*'s selectNodes() method to get a list of matches. Everything else is just output and error handling.

4.5 XSLT

Now, what exactly is XSLT? It's a way to transform an XML document into XHTML, plain old ASCII, or pretty much anything else. XSLT can add, remove, or rearrange elements; it also includes conditionals, loops, and many (but not all) of the other things you'd expect from a programming language.

XSLT's execution model is different from most programming languages. Instead of executing statements one after another, XSLT tries to match its input against a *template*. When a match is found, XSLT transforms the part of the source document that matched the template to create some output. Parts that didn't match the template are copied through to the output unchanged. This match-and-replace cycle is executed over and over, until nothing left in the document matches any of the available templates. Suppose that we have information about the developers working for a small consulting firm in an XML file like this:

```xml
<?xml version="1.0" encoding="ISO-8859-1"?>
<personnel>
  <person>
    <surname>Hopper</surname>
    <forename>Grace</forename>
    <email>ghopper@pragprog.com</email>
    <start-date year="2004" month="9" day="15"/>
    <rate>320.00</rate>
    <skill name="C++" proficiency="3"/>
    <skill name="Python" proficiency="3"/>
    <skill name="management" proficiency="2"/>
  </person>
  <person>
    <surname>Babbage</surname>
    <forename>Chuck</forename>
    <email>cb@pragprog.uk</email>
    <start-date year="1820" month="3" day="1"/>
    <rate currency="GBP">125.00</rate>
    <skill name="Fortran" proficiency="2"/>
    <skill name="math" proficiency="4"/>
    <skill name="Python" proficiency="1"/>
  </person>
  <person>
    <surname>Turing</surname>
    <forename>Al</forename>
    <email>at@pragprog.uk</email>
    <start-date year="1946" month="7" day="3"/>
    <rate currency="GBP">245.00</rate>
    <skill name="Fortran" proficiency="2"/>
    <skill name="math" proficiency="4"/>
    <skill name="management" proficiency="0"/>
  </person>
</personnel>
```

We want to create a web page showing the names and email addresses of everyone in the company. The transformation is pretty simple: create a table, and add one row to it for each *<person>* in the input. Here's how to do it in XSLT:

```xml
<?xml version="1.0" encoding="ISO-8859-1"?>
<xsl:stylesheet version="1.0"
 xmlns:xsl="http://www.w3.org/1999/XSL/Transform">
<xsl:template match="/personnel">
  <!-- Start of boilerplate HTML output -->
  <html>
  <body>
    <h1>Personnel</h1>
    <table border="1">
      <tr>
        <th align="left">Forename</th>
        <th align="left">Surname</th>
        <th align="left">Email</th>
      </tr>
      <!-- Repeat this section for each person -->
      <xsl:for-each select="person">
      <tr>
        <!-- Select specific fields for each person -->
        <td><xsl:value-of select="forename"/></td>
        <td><xsl:value-of select="surname"/></td>
        <td><xsl:value-of select="email"/></td>
      </tr>
      </xsl:for-each>
    <!-- Close the document -->
    </table>
  </body>
  </html>
</xsl:template>
</xsl:stylesheet>
```

This XSLT file has four parts:

- The outer wrapper, which consists of the XML and *<xsl:stylesheet>* declarations. Every XSLT template must include these.

- The *<xsl:template>* declaration, which specifies what this template matches. The value of the *<match>* attribute is an XPath expression that specifies what we want the template applied to. In this case, we want it to match the root *<personnel>* element.

- Some HTML that is to be copied directly into the output. Here, this consists of the page title, the table's header and footer, and the table's title row. These lines are copied verbatim during processing.

- A *<xsl:for-each>*, which creates an implicit loop over all the *<person>* elements below *<personnel>*.

Here's what happens when an XSLT processor applies this template to our personnel list:

1. */personnel* matches the document's root element.

2. The processor scans the body of the template, copying HTML tags as it goes, until it finds the *<xsl:for-each>*.

3. The argument to the *<xsl:for-each>*'s select= attribute tells the processor to copy the material inside the loop to the output once for each *<person>* element below the current element (which is still *<personnel>*).

4. The HTML tags inside the *<xsl:for-each>* are copied once each for Grace Hopper, Chuck Babbage, and Al Turing. Each time, the *<xsl:value-of>*s are replaced by the text values of their *<forename>*, *<surname>*, and *<email>* elements.

5. The loop ends, and the remaining fixed elements of the template are copied to the output.

The output is

```
<html><body>
<h1>Personnel</h1>
<table border="1">
<tr>
<th align="left">Forename</th>
<th align="left">Surname</th>
<th align="left">Email</th>
</tr>
<tr>
<td>Grace</td>
<td>Hopper</td>
<td>ghopper@pragprog.com</td>
</tr>
<tr>
<td>Chuck</td>
<td>Babbage</td>
<td>cb@pragprog.uk</td>
</tr>
<tr>
<td>Al</td>
<td>Turing</td>
<td>at@pragprog.uk</td>
</tr>
</table>
</body></html>
```

Selecting Particular Elements

All right, what if we just want a list of our most expensive consultants?

As we saw in the previous section, XPath supports numerical comparisons, so we can modify the template to select only those people whose rate is greater than some threshold (say, $300/hr).

The template is shown in the next listing:

```
<?xml version="1.0" encoding="ISO-8859-1"?>
<xsl:stylesheet version="1.0"
 xmlns:xsl="http://www.w3.org/1999/XSL/Transform">

<xsl:template match="/personnel">

  <html>
  <body>
    <h1>Expensive Personnel</h1>
    <table border="1">
      <tr>
        <th align="left">Forename</th>
        <th align="left">Surname</th>
        <th align="left">Rate</th>
      </tr>

      <xsl:for-each select="person[rate &gt; 300]">
        <tr>
          <td><xsl:value-of select="forename"/></td>
          <td><xsl:value-of select="surname"/></td>
          <td><xsl:value-of select="rate"/></td>
        </tr>
      </xsl:for-each>

    </table>
  </body>
  </html>

</xsl:template>
</xsl:stylesheet>
```

(Notice, by the way, that the greater-than operator has to be written *>*, since the XSLT stylesheet must itself be legal XML.) Sure enough, its output contains just a single line for Grace Hopper:

```
<html><body>
<h1>Expensive Personnel</h1>
<table border="1">
<tr>
<th align="left">Forename</th>
<th align="left">Surname</th>
<th align="left">Rate</th>
</tr>
<tr>
<td>Grace</td>
<td>Hopper</td>
<td>320.00</td>
</tr>
</table>
</body></html>
```

But wait a second: when we're looking for expensive consultants, shouldn't we take currency exchange rates into account? Al's £245/hr isn't actually less than our threshold of $300/hr; if we convert from British pounds to American dollars, he's actually the most expensive person on staff.

All right, we're programmers; we know how to do this. Let's multiply each consultant's rate by a conversion factor based on the currency it was quoted in and then check the result against our threshold. Simple, right?

Not quite. Let's take a look at how XSLT does conditionals. Suppose we want to highlight those consultants who charge in British pounds, rather than American dollars.

We use *<xsl:choose>* to open an *if/else* block, and then use *<xsl:when>* to test various conditions. We can also use *<xsl:otherwise>* to implement default handling, just as we could put an *else* at the end of a sequence of *if* and *elif* statements in Python. The resulting template is

```
<xsl:for-each select="person">
  <tr>
    <td><xsl:value-of select="forename"/></td>
    <td><xsl:value-of select="surname"/></td>
    <xsl:choose>
      <xsl:when test="rate/@currency='GBP'">
        <td color="#020202"><xsl:value-of select="rate"/></td>
      </xsl:when>
      <xsl:otherwise>
        <td><xsl:value-of select="rate"/></td>
      </xsl:otherwise>
    </xsl:choose>
  </tr>
</xsl:for-each>
```

Great! Now all we have to do is convert British rates into American dollars and use that value instead of the raw rate. But how do we do that?

First, declare the conversion rate. We can do this anywhere, but it's simplest to put it at the top of the template:

```
<xsl:variable name="poundsToDollars" select="1.85"/>
```

(Yes, you really do set the value using the select= attribute.)

Second, create a temporary variable inside the *<xsl:for-each>* loop, whose value is either the raw rate in dollars or that rate times our conversion factor if the rate is quoted in pounds.

The syntax is

```
<xsl:variable name="actualRate">
  <xsl:choose>
    <xsl:when test="rate/@currency='GBP'">
      <xsl:value-of select="rate*$poundsToDollars"/>
    </xsl:when>
    <xsl:otherwise>
      <xsl:value-of select="rate"/>
    </xsl:otherwise>
  </xsl:choose>
</xsl:variable>
```

This is equivalent to the (much simpler) pseudo-C:

```
actualRate = (rate.currency == 'GBP') ? (rate * poundsToDollars) : rate;
```

The $ symbol that appears in front of *poundsToDollars* is very important. This tells XSLT that we want the value of a local variable and not a value out of the XML input.

In fact, you'll notice that we have to use a $ further down as well, when we test *actualRate*'s value:

```
<xsl:if test="$actualRate &gt; 300">
  <tr>
    <td><xsl:value-of select="forename"/></td>
    <td><xsl:value-of select="surname"/></td>
    <td><xsl:value-of select="rate"/></td>
  </tr>
</xsl:if>
```

The whole thing is

```
<?xml version="1.0" encoding="ISO-8859-1"?>
<xsl:stylesheet version="1.0"
 xmlns:xsl="http://www.w3.org/1999/XSL/Transform">

<xsl:variable name="poundsToDollars" select="1.85"/>

<xsl:template match="/personnel">

  <html>
  <body>
    <h1>Expensive Personnel</h1>
    <table border="1">
      <tr>
        <th align="left">Forename</th>
        <th align="left">Surname</th>
        <th align="left">Rate</th>
      </tr>

      <xsl:for-each select="person">

        <xsl:variable name="actualRate">
          <xsl:choose>
            <xsl:when test="rate/@currency='GBP'">
              <xsl:value-of select="rate*$poundsToDollars"/>
            </xsl:when>
            <xsl:otherwise>
              <xsl:value-of select="rate"/>
            </xsl:otherwise>
          </xsl:choose>
        </xsl:variable>

        <xsl:if test="$actualRate &gt; 300">
          <tr>
            <td><xsl:value-of select="forename"/></td>
            <td><xsl:value-of select="surname"/></td>
            <td><xsl:value-of select="rate"/></td>
          </tr>
        </xsl:if>

      </xsl:for-each>

    </table>
  </body>
  </html>

</xsl:template>
</xsl:stylesheet>
```

Using Multiple Templates

There's another way to tackle complex processing in XSLT, one that is often easier to read (although that's not saying much). Instead of squeezing everything into one template, you can define several templates, each of which matches something specific. The body of that template can then invoke template application recursively so that you can handle each part of the input separately.

For example, suppose we want to print our staff list like this:

```
<html><body>
<dl>
<dt><b>Hopper</b>, Grace</dt>
<dd>ghopper@pragprog.com<br>320.00</dd>
<dt><b>Babbage</b>, Chuck</dt>
<dd>cb@pragprog.uk<br>125.00(pounds sterling)</dd>
<dt><b>Turing</b>, Al</dt>
<dd>at@pragprog.uk<br>245.00(pounds sterling)</dd>
</dl>
</body></html>
```

We start by defining a template that matches the root *<personnel>* node of the input and produces the skeleton of the output:

```
<xsl:template match="/personnel">
  <html>
  <body>
  <dl>
    <xsl:apply-templates/>
  </dl>
  </body>
  </html>
</xsl:template>
```

The key part of this template is the *<xsl:apply-templates>* element in its middle, which tells the XSLT processor to process each of the current node's children on its own. If the XSLT file contained only this one template, there'd be little point in doing this. But we can put a second template in the same XSLT file, like this:

```
<xsl:template match="person">
  <dt><b><xsl:value-of select="surname"/></b>,
      <xsl:value-of select="forename"/></dt>
  <dd>
  <xsl:apply-templates select="email"/>
  <br/>
  <xsl:apply-templates select="rate"/>
  </dd>
</xsl:template>
```

This template matches *<person>* nodes, which are (funnily enough) exactly what we get when we recurse over *<personnel>*'s children. After copying the person's surname and forename to the output, this template invokes processing on the *<person>*'s *<email>* and *<rate>* children. The following two templates handle these:

```
<xsl:template match="email">
  <xsl:value-of select="."/>
</xsl:template>
<xsl:template match="rate">
  <xsl:value-of select="."/>
  <xsl:if test="@currency='GBP'">(pounds sterling)</xsl:if>
</xsl:template>
```

Notice, by the way, that the template that matches rates uses *<xsl:if>*. This tag is a simplified version of *<xsl:choose>* and *<xsl:when>* that tests a single condition.

How a Real XSLT Programmer Would Do It

The XSLT templates we built up in the preceding sections work, but they aren't what an experienced XSLT programmer would do. Industrial-strength XSLT is usually written in a functional programming style, free from assignment and explicit control. For example, here's Dave Thomas's solution:

```
Line 1  <?xml version="1.0" encoding="ISO-8859-1"?>
        <xsl:stylesheet version="1.0"
                        xmlns:xsl="http://www.w3.org/1999/XSL/Transform">

5         <xsl:template match="/personnel">
            <table>
              <xsl:apply-templates />
            </table>
          </xsl:template>
10
          <xsl:template match="person">
            <tr>
              <td>
                <xsl:value-of select="./surname"/>
15            </td>
              <td>
                <xsl:apply-templates select="./rate"/>
              </td>
            </tr>
20        </xsl:template>

          <xsl:variable name="exchange-rate"
                        select="document('rates.xml')/*/rate" />

25        <xsl:template match="rate">

            <xsl:variable name="currency">
              <xsl:choose>
                <xsl:when test="@currency">
30                <xsl:value-of select="@currency"/>
                </xsl:when>
                <xsl:otherwise>USD</xsl:otherwise>
              </xsl:choose>
            </xsl:variable>
35
            <xsl:variable name="rate">
              <xsl:value-of select="$exchange-rate[@currency=$currency]/@rate" />
            </xsl:variable>

40          <xsl:value-of select=". * $rate" />
          </xsl:template>
        </xsl:stylesheet>
```

This template depends on a lookup table stored in a separate file called rates.xml:

```
<?xml version ="1.0" encoding="ISO-8859-1" ?>
<rates>
  <rate currency ="USD" rate="1.00" />
  <rate currency ="GBP" rate="1.85" />
</rates>
```

Line 17 inserts a rate in U.S. dollars into the output document. This rate is calculated by the bit of template on line 36, which in turn uses the lookup table loaded on line 22. There is no explicit loop, and if a new currency has to be added to the mix, only rates.xml has to be changed. It takes a bit of getting used to, but if you're going to be processing a lot of XML, it's worth the effort; [Man02] is an excellent place to start.

4.6 Summary

As I said a few pages ago, I don't like XSLT very much. If all you want to do is rearrange the nodes in a tree, it's useful, if rather verbose. As soon as I want to do any serious data crunching, though, I find myself switching to other tools.

Luckily, XML is still young enough that the number of other tools is constantly growing. Recent versions of Python, for example, include the xml.pulldom library, which combines some of the best features of SAX and DOM. Like DOM, it builds a tree in memory, so programmers don't have to write event-driven code. Unlike DOM, however, it doesn't build the whole tree at once. Instead, it "pulls" just enough data from the incoming stream to build a user-selected portion of the document being parsed. This makes pulldom faster and reduces its memory demands.

Another newish API is ElementTree, which has both a pure Python and a mixed C/Python implementation (http://effbot.org/zone/celementtree.htm). As with DOM, ElementTree represents XML documents as trees in memory. However, ElementTree doesn't try to stick to DOM's C-inspired conventions.

Instead, it represents nodes using a class called Element, which is a cross between a list and a dictionary. Each Element has

- a tag that identifies the element's type,

- a dictionary of attributes,

- a list of children, and

- some text.

That's it: no superfluous classes, just simple, lightweight objects. And as a bonus, Element's methods can search for nodes that match certain patterns using a subset of XPath. Here's a simple example that parses a document and prints out all the emphasized text:

```
import sys
from elementtree import ElementTree
root = ElementTree.parse(sys.stdin)
for node in root.findall(".//em"):
    print node.text
```

On the downside, ElementTree isn't part of the standard library and isn't as well documented as either SAX or DOM. If you have a lot of crunching to do, though, its simplicity may outweigh these factors.

With that in mind, here are a few things to remember when crunching XML:

- Keep it legal! Don't use the fact that browsers can display badly formatted HTML as an excuse to omit closing tags or skip the quotes around attributes—you'll just be creating headaches for yourself, or whoever inherits your work.

- Use SAX when the documents you're processing are large and the processing itself is simple.

- Use XSLT when you're transforming one XML document into another according to fairly simple rules.

- If you need real data structures or complex conditional logic, or have to work with data from some other source as well (such as a relational database), you'll probably need the full power of a real programming language, such as Python or Java. When you do, DOM is your friend.

- Remember that you can use XPath in a program *without* using XSLT, just as you would use regular expressions. In particular, using XPath to find things and DOM to transform them is a very powerful combination.

- This is the least mature of the areas covered in this book and hence the one that is changing most rapidly. You should therefore stay on the lookout for newer and better tools.

Chapter 5

Binary Data

When you get right down to it, all data is stored as ones and zeroes. Those ones and zeroes either represent characters that can be displayed as human-readable text by an editor like Notepad, or something else. That "something else" is (misleadingly) called *binary data*.

There are three reasons why people use binary data:

- Speed. It takes dozens of machine operations to "add" the integer represented by the string *123* to the one represented by *456*. If the values are stored as binary integers, on the other hand, it can be done in one instruction.

- Size. Storing 10239472 as a string takes 8 bytes,[1] but storing it as a binary integer takes only 4. As an extreme case, Boolean values can be represented in a single bit each, while the strings *true* and *false* need 32 and 40 bits respectively.

- Lack of anything better. PostScript is proof that you can store some kinds of graphics as text,[2] but it is inefficient for raster images. In theory, you could store music and video as text, too, but such a scheme would be fat, slow, and at least as hard to process as MP3, MPEG, and similar binary formats.

So, why not use binary? One reason is portability: as we'll see, different computers store numbers in different ways, so a file created on one machine may look (or sound) like gibberish on another.

Another reason is that every time you invent a new way to store data, you have to build a new set of tools to manipulate it. Just as you can't usefully view binary

---

[1] In 8-bit ASCII. If you're using Unicode, it can take up to 32.

[2] In fact, PostScript files are programs whose instructions re-create the image.

> \\/ **Joe Asks...**
> ?ς
> ⁀ **When Should I Do This?**
> _____
>
> You should write code to crunch binary data only as a last resort, since there are lots of good libraries around for processing common binary formats. If you're working with images, for example, the Python Imaging Library (`http://www.pythonware.com/products/pil/`) handles JPEG, GIF, PNG, and many others, while if you're working with sound, MP3 libraries are as common as sticky Return keys. If you can't find what you need, though, the tools and techniques described in this chapter will be your friends.

data with conventional text editors, you usually can't manipulate it with regular expressions, XML parsers, and other generic tools. This chapter looks at what you have to do instead.

5.1 Numbers

Let's start by looking at how integers are represented in computer memory. As you probably already know, positive numbers are stored using base-2: 9_{10} is 1001_2, or $(1\times2^3)+(0\times2^2)+(0\times2^1)+(1\times2^0)$, just as 1001_{10} is $(1\times10^3)+(0\times10^2)+(0\times10^1)+(1\times10^0)$. (Remember, X^0 is 1 for every X.)

What about negative numbers? Some early computers used a sign-and-value representation, in which the first bit of the integer was 0 for positive numbers and 1 for negative ones. With this representation, 0011_2 is 3_{10}, but 1011_2 is -3_{10}.

Sign-and-value is easy for human beings to read but awkward for digital circuits to handle. It also has both a positive zero, 0000, and a negative zero, 1000, which makes arithmetic complicated. Almost all modern computers therefore use a scheme called *two's complement*. Like an old-fashioned mechanical odometer, two's complement "rolls over" when it goes below 0, so -1_{10} is represented as 1111_2, -2_{10} as 1110_2, -3_{10} as 1101_2, and so on. 1000_2 is then the most negative number ($-(2^{N-1})$ if N bits are being used), while 0111 ($2^{N-1}-1$) is the most positive.

Two's complement can also roll over when numbers become too large. For example, suppose you add 7_{10} and 2_{10} on a machine that stores number in only 4 bits. 7_{10} is 0111_2, and 2_{10} is 0010_2, so the answer is 1001_2. This isn't 9_{10}, though; it's -7_{10}. Oops.

What *actually* happens when you go over the top (or under the bottom) when doing arithmetic depends on your language and your machine. Some systems just let it happen; others raise an exception, or let you set flags to specify which behavior you want.

Some languages choose a different route. When your integers become too large to fit in a single word, for example, Python automatically switches to a multiword "long integer" format. This uses as many 32-bit words of memory as the value requires. Long integers are displayed with a trailing *L*, as shown by the following interactive Python session:

```
>>> x = 0x7FFFFFFF      # Largest positive signed 32-bit integer
>>> x                   # Show it
2147483647
>>> x + 1               # Show the next-highest integer
2147483648L
```

Why not use long integers all the time? Because arithmetic on them uses functions, rather than single instructions, which slows things down a lot.

Notation

For some reason, only a handful of programming languages let you to write numbers in binary, but most let you use octal (base-8) and hexadecimal (base-16) notation. Octal numbers are written using the digits 0–7; each digit represents three bits (Figure 5.1 on the next page). In C and its offspring, you indicate that a number is in octal with a leading 0, so *0751* represents 111101001_2, or 489_{10}.

Hexadecimal (or hex) numbers start with the prefix *0x* or *0X*, and use the letters a–f (or A–F) to represent the digits from 10 to 15. For example, *0x07* is the same as 7_{10}, and *0x09* is 9_{10}, but the next largest number is *0x0A*, which is 10_{10}. Figure 5.1 on the following page shows the values of the other "extra" hex digits. The value *0x97C2*, for example, represents 1001011111000010_2 (or 38850_{10}), while 01011010_2 can be broken into two groups of four to give *(0101)(1010)*, or *0x5A*.

Hex is more widely used than octal these days, primarily because two hex digits correspond exactly to one 8-bit byte, while two octal digits are too little (6 bits), and three are too much (9 bits). One common use for hex is to encode colors in HTML. Most modern displays use 8 bits for each of the red, green, and blue components of the color, which means that six hex digits can be used to represent any color. Pure red is *0xFF0000* (all the red bits are one, all the green and blue bits are zero); half-strength gray is *0x808080* (red, green, and blue each at half their peak value), while *0xFF80FF* is a rather medicinal pink (red and blue maxed out, green half as strong).

Binary	Octal	Decimal	Hex
0000	00	0	0x00
0001	01	1	0x01
0010	02	2	0x02
0011	03	3	0x03
0100	04	4	0x04
0101	05	5	0x05
0110	06	6	0x06
0111	07	7	0x07
1000		8	0x08
1001		9	0x09
1010			0x0a
1011			0x0b
1100			0x0c
1101			0x0d
1110			0x0e
1111			0x0f

Figure 5.1: BINARY, OCTAL, DECIMAL, AND HEXADECIMAL

Bitwise Operations

Almost all languages provide four bit-level operations for working with binary values: and, or, xor, and not, written &, |, ^, and ~ respectively. The similarities between these names and the names of the standard Boolean operators is no accident: if you think of 1 as being true and 0 as being false, then the bitwise operators return the same answers as their logical counterparts.

A	B	A & B	A | B	A ^ B
0	0	0	0	0
0	1	0	1	1
1	0	0	1	1
1	1	1	1	0

A	~A
0	1
1	0

As these tables show, & (and) yields a 1 only if both its arguments are 1's, just as logical AND is true only if both is arguments are true. | (or) yields 1 if either or both of its arguments are 1, while ^ (exclusive-or, or xor) yields 1 if either argument is

1, but *not* if both are; it is equivalent to the English phrase either/or. Finally, ~ (not) flips its argument: 1 becomes 0, and 0 becomes 1.

When these operators are applied to multibit values, they work on each corresponding pair of bits independently. For example:

1100	&	0110	=	0100	
1100	|	0110	=	1110	
1100	^	0110	=	1010	
	~	0110	=	1001	

You can use and, or, and not to set or clear individual bits. In order to set a particular bit, create a string of bits in which that bit is 1 and all the other bits are 0. When this is or'd with a value, the bit you care about is guaranteed to come out 1, while all of the other bits will be left as they are.

Conversely, if you want to set a bit to zero, create a value in which that bit is 0 and all the others are 1; and'ing it with another value will clear the bit in question and leave the others as they were. Since *11110111* is hard to read, it's common to create a value with a single 1, negate it (to convert ones to zeroes and vice versa), and then use that:

```
mask = ~ 0x0100  # binary 1111 1110 1111 1111
val = val & mask #     clears this ^ bit
```

Shifting

The other bit-level operation that most languages provide is *shifting*. As the name suggests, shifting just moves bits left or right a few places. If you shift the bit pattern 0110_2 left one place, it becomes 1100_2, while if you shift it right, it becomes 0011_2. Shifting X left by Y places is written X<<Y, while shifting right is written X>>Y.

Just as shifting a decimal number left a place corresponds to multiplying by 10 (as when 33_{10} becomes 330_{10}), shifting a binary number left one place is the same as multiplying it by 2. For example, if you shift 0110_2 (which is 6_{10}) left, it becomes 1100_2, or 12_{10}. Despite persistent folklore, shifting is not much more efficient than integer division on today's machines: *x*4* is only a few nanoseconds slower than *x<<2* on a modern processor, but easier to read everywhere.

Conversely, shifting a number right corresponds to dividing by 2 and throwing away the remainder. For example, 7_{10}>>1 is 0111_2>>1, which is 0011_2, or 3_{10}.

But what happens if the top bit of an integer changes from 1 to 0, or vice versa, as a result of shifting? Suppose we're programming a 4-bit microcontroller, which can represent values from -8_{10} (1000_2 if we're using two's complement) to 7_{10} (0111_2). On this machine, 6_{10}<<1 is 1100_2, but this is -4_{10}, not 12_{10}.

In this case, the wrong answer is mostly our fault: there's no way to represent 12_{10} as a signed 4-bit integer, so what we tried to do was illegal. But what about shifting right? 1100_2 is -4_{10} in two's complement; shifting right gives us 0110_2, or 6_{10}, instead of the 1110_2 (-2_{10}) we "should" get.

This problem is an example of what Joel Spolsky calls *leaky abstractions*[Spo04]. Left shift and right shift aren't actually multiplication and division; they do act like them most of the time, but every once in a while, reality leaks through.

Different languages deal with this particular problem in different ways. Java's solution is to provide two versions of right shift: >>, which fills in the high end with zeroes, and >>>, which copies in the topmost (sign) bit of the original value. The latter gives the right answer when working with signed integers but would do the wrong thing if the integers were unsigned (i.e., if all N bits were used to represent values from 0 to 2^N-1).

The other "solution" (and I use that term advisedly) is to leave it up to the underlying hardware. C (and by extension C++, Python, and several other languages) does this, which means that if you want to be sure of getting a particular answer, no matter what hardware your program is running on, you have to handle the top bit yourself. In Python, for example, you can use the following to shift right safely:

```
def rshift(val):
    if val & 0x8000:
        result = 0x8000 | (val >> 1)
    else:
        result = 0x7FFF & (val >> 1)
    return result
```

5.2 Input and Output

Every language has libraries for reading and writing bytes directly. In Python, for example, files and their kin (including sockets) have two methods: write(S), which writes the bytes contained in the string S to the file, and read(N), which reads up to the next N bytes. If there are fewer than N bytes left in the file, read() returns as many as it can; subsequent calls return an empty string to signal that the end of the file has been reached. For example, the following program copies a file one 128-byte block at a time:

```
import sys
input = open(sys.argv[1], 'r')
output = open(sys.argv[2], 'w')
while True:
    block = input.read(128)
    if not block:
        break
    output.write(block)
input.close()
output.close()
```

At least, it's supposed to: if you run it on Windows and give it a file that was created on Unix, you may find that the output isn't quite the same as the input. The reason is that some I/O libraries on Windows try to be clever and convert each newline character to a carriage return plus a newline—in other words, convert Unix-style line endings to their Windows-style equivalents. This is helpful when you're processing text but is an unkind thing to do to an image file. To turn this feature off, you must open the input file in binary mode in Python (other languages have similar modes) by using *rb* instead of *r* (or *wb* instead of *w* if you're writing).

Packing and Unpacking

In C and C++, any structure (or object) that contains only primitive values like Booleans, integers, and floating-point numbers is stored in a single contiguous block of memory. This makes it easy to write a simple *struct* to a file, since all you have to do is copy a block of bytes. For example, the fwrite() function in C's stdio library takes four arguments—a pointer, a count of how many structures you want to write, the size of each structure in bytes, and an open file—and copies bytes from memory to the file:

```c
#include <stdio.h>
#define NUM_COL 3
typedef struct {
  unsigned char red;
  unsigned char green;
  unsigned char blue;
} color;

int main(int argc, char ** argv) {
  color * primary = NULL;
  FILE * output = NULL;
  int i, len;

  /* Create primary colors. */
  primary = (color *)malloc(NUM_COL * sizeof(color));
  primary[0].red   = 0xFF;
  primary[1].green = 0xFF;
  primary[2].blue  = 0xFF;

  /* Write to file. */
  output = fopen(argv[1], "w");
  fwrite(primary, sizeof(color), NUM_COL, output);
  fclose(output);

  /* Put our toys away. */
  free(primary);
}
```

Once data is in a file, you can use the Unix command od -x to look at it:[3]

```
0000000 00ff 0000 00ff 0000 00ff
0000011
```

---

[3]od stands for "octal dump," since by default, it displays data in octal. These days, most programmers use the -x flag to tell it to display values in hexadecimal.

B   Unsigned integer (8-bit byte)
c   Single character (string of length 1)
d   Double (64 bits)
f   Float (32 bits)
h   Short integer (16 bits)
i   Integer (32 bits)
s   String (handled specially)
x   Single padding byte (no value)

Figure 5.2: PACKING FORMATS

Life is a little more difficult (but a whole lot safer) in other languages, which don't let you muck with memory quite so directly. Instead, you have to pack the values contained in your data structures into a contiguous byte array, then write that out, and then reverse the process for input.

In Perl, you use the pack() and unpack() functions. In Python, you use methods with the same names from the struct module. When packing, you provide a *format specification* that specifies how you want the values treated. Just like the format strings used in C's printf(), a packing format specifies the types and sizes of the items you're packing. Together, these values specify exactly how much memory the packed data will occupy.

Let's take a closer look at Python's functions:

- pack(format, v1, v2, ...) packs the values *v1*, *v2*, etc., according to *format*, and returns a string of bytes.
- unpack(format, str) unpacks the values in *str* according to *format*, returning the values found.
- calcsize(format) determines how many bytes the data described by *format* will occupy.

Figure 5.2 lists the characters you can put in a format string and what they mean. Any format specifier can be preceded by a decimal count to signal multiple items of that type. The format *4i*, for example, specifies four integers, while *10cf* specifies ten characters followed by a single floating-point number.

So, let's pack the integer 3 as an 8-bit, a 16-bit, and a 32-bit integer:

```
from struct import pack, unpack
for format in ["B", "h", "i"]:
  s = pack(format, 3)
  print format, ":", repr(s)
```

Joe Asks...

What's with the \x's?

Some control characters, like tab and newline, are used so often that C (and its descendents, including Java and Python) provide ways to represent them. Others, which have names like *data link escape* (10_{16}) and *negative acknowledge* (15_{10}), aren't that important. In Python, they are represented using hexadecimal escape sequences, such as *\x10\x15*. While I can't think of any good reason to put such characters in a URL, you can do it using the % escapes discussed in Section 7.2, *URL Encoding*, on page 176, as in %10%15.

The program's output is

```
b : '\x03'
h : '\x03\x00'
i : '\x03\x00\x00\x00'
```

Hmm...Each result is the expected size—8, 16, or 32 bits—but shouldn't the 16-bit result be 0003 (in hex) rather than 0300? And what about the 32-bit result—shouldn't it be 00000003?

Well, it turns out that the answer depends on whether you're using a *big-endian* or a *little-endian* machine.[4] In a big-endian system, the most significant byte in an integer is stored at the first (i.e., lowest) address in memory. In a little-endian system, the least significant byte is stored first.

For example, if we store the 32-bit integer 1027_{10} (which is $0x0407_{16}$) on a big-endian machine starting at address 8000, its four bytes are laid out like this:

```
8000    0x00
8001    0x00
8002    0x04
8003    0x07
```

Store the same value on a little-endian machine, and it is

---

[4]The terms come from *Gulliver's Travels*; the hot political issue in his imaginary land of Lilliput was whether eggs should be opened at the big or the little end.

```
8000   0x07
8001   0x04
8002   0x00
8003   0x00
```

The Intel chips used in modern PCs are little-endian. Motorola processors, on the other hand, are big-endian, so if you save values on one type of machine and move them to another, you may have to reorder the bytes in order to get the right results.

Back to our example. Suppose you want to look at the bytes inside a floating-point number. (I know, I know, but suppose you did....) You can't do this:

```
5.2 & 0x000000FF
```

to extract the lowest 8 bits, because & and other bitwise operators aren't defined on floating-point values. Instead, you have to pack the float into 4 bytes and then unpack those bytes as unsigned 8-bit integers, like this:

```
from struct import pack, unpack
s = pack("f", 5.02e23)
bytes = unpack("4B", s)
for i in range(len(bytes)):
  print "%d: %02x" % (i, bytes[i])
```

This program's output is

```
0:  f3
1:  9a
2:  d4
3:  66
```

Note the loop: it's needed because unpack() always returns a list of values (since most formats specify more than one item).

This example illustrates that bytes mean what you want them to mean, nothing more and nothing less. Want to know what value the bytes in the string *fish* represent as an integer? Try running unpack("i", "fish"); the answer is 1752394086_{10}.

These examples show that your computer has no magical way of knowing what you mean by a particular sequence of bytes. It's up to you to make sure that when you unpack data, you use the same format that was used to pack it. If you don't, you'll get values of some kind, but probably not the values you expected.

5.3 Strings

Figure 5.2 on page 124 says that s is used to pack strings, but they must be handled specially, since their length can vary. In order to pack a string, we must tell the library how long it is; in order to unpack one, we must tell the library how many bytes to read from the packed representation.

Here's an example:

```
from struct import pack, unpack
format = "9s"
original = "pragmatic"
data = pack(format, original)
print repr(data)
duplicate = unpack(format, data)
print duplicate[0]
```

Its output is

```
'pragmatic'
pragmatic
```

That was easy: nine bytes in, nine bytes out. But what happens if the string is longer, or shorter, than the 9 bytes we've specified in the format? Here's a four-character example:

```
from struct import pack, unpack
format = "4s"
for original in ["a", "aa", "aaaa", "aaaaaaaa"]:
    data = pack(format, original)
    duplicate = unpack(format, data)
    print original, "=>", repr(data), "=>", duplicate[0]
```

It produces

```
a => 'a\x00\x00\x00' => a
aa => 'aa\x00\x00' => aa
aaaa => 'aaaa' => aaaa
aaaaaaaa => 'aaaa' => aaaa
```

That doesn't seem so bad: when there isn't enough data to satisfy the format, pack() fills in the blanks with zero bytes.

But what about unpacking? Let's take a closer look by having Python print out exactly what's in the string that unpack() returns:

```
from struct import pack, unpack
format = "4s"
for original in ["a", "aa", "aaaa", "aaaaaaaa"]:
    data = pack(format, original)
    duplicate = unpack(format, data)
    print original, "=>", repr(data), "=>", `duplicate[0]`
```

This produces

```
a => 'a\x00\x00\x00' => 'a\x00\x00\x00'
aa => 'aa\x00\x00' => 'aa\x00\x00'
aaaa => 'aaaa' => 'aaaa'
aaaaaaaa => 'aaaa' => 'aaaa'
```

Storing Strings

Different programming languages use two fundamentally different ways to store strings. Pascal's is to store a count, followed by that many characters. C, on the other hand, stores a *sentinel*—a byte with the value 0—at the end of the string.

C's approach uses less memory per string and doesn't put an upper limit on how long strings can be. (If you use two bytes to store the string's length, for example, no string can be longer than $2^{16}-1$ characters long.) With Pascal's, on the other hand, you don't have to scan a string to find out how big it is, and you can put zero bytes inside strings without getting confused.

The biggest difference, though, is that Pascal's approach is safer, since it allows a program to stop you from accidentally overwriting memory that's 1,923,742 characters beyond the end of a six-character string. Doing this is the basis of *buffer overflow attacks*, which are one of the most common ways to break into machines. For this reason, Java, Python, and most other modern languages use the Pascal approach, but you have to understand, and be able to convert to, C's in order to use legacy code.

Whoops: the output isn't actually the same as the input. unpack() has kept the zero bytes that pack() inserted as filler; they just don't show up on the screen when we print the string.

unpack() isn't doing anything wrong here. In fact, what else could it do? It didn't know that the zero bytes in its input weren't part of the original string.

In order to get the right answer, we have to store the length of the string explicitly when packing it, so that when we unpack it, we know how many bytes to use. This is also the best way to handle other variable-length structures, such as arrays: store the number of elements in the structure in a value whose size is known (such as a 32-bit integer), and then store that many instances of the structure's basic type.

Suppose, for example, that we want to store a list of integers. We can write a function packIntVec() that stores the list's length as an integer and then appends the packed representation of each integer to that:

```python
def packVec(vec):
    buf = pack("i", len(vec))
    for v in vec:
        buf += pack("i", v)
    return buf
```

The complementary function unpackIntVec() is a little more complicated, but only a little. It uses calcsize() to find out how many bytes an integer takes up, slices that many bytes off the front of the packed data to find out how many integers there are, and then grabs those integers one by one:

```
def unpackVec(buf):
    size = calcsize("i")
    num = unpack("i", buf[0:size])[0]
    pos = size
    result = []
    for i in range(num):
        v = unpack("i", buf[pos:pos+size])
        result.append(v[0])
        pos += size
    return result
```

Here are a few simple tests:

```
if __name__ == "__main__":
    tests = [
        [],
        [1],
        [19, 27],
        [-3, 456]
    ]
    for t in tests:
        data = packVec(t)
        print repr(data)
        result = unpackVec(data)
        assert result == t
```

Their output is

```
'\x00\x00\x00\x00'
'\x01\x00\x00\x00\x01\x00\x00\x00'
'\x02\x00\x00\x00\x13\x00\x00\x00\x1b\x00\x00\x00'
'\x02\x00\x00\x00\xfd\xff\xff\xff\xc8\x01\x00\x00'
```

Note: you should *never* actually write your packing function this way, since repeatedly appending strings to one another inside a loop is very inefficient. It's better to append data to a buffer, rather than concatenating strings repeatedly:

```
from cStringIO import StringIO
def packVec(vec):
    buf = StringIO()
    buf.write(pack("i", len(vec)))
    for v in vec:
        buf.write(pack("i", v))
    return buf.getvalue()
```

Alternatively, you can build a list of string fragments and then join them all together at the end:

```
def packVec(vec):
    buf = [pack("i", len(vec))]
    for v in vec:
        buf.append(pack("i", v))
    return ''.join(buf)
```

This concern with performance may seem to fly in the face of earlier advice not to worry about it, but repeated string concatenation is a bad habit that you can easily train yourself to avoid.

Variable-Length Data and Variable Formats

Packing a size, followed by that many items of that size, allows us to do things we couldn't do before. If we have a list of strings, for example, we can store the length of the list first and then store each string as a size+data pair, as if it were a mini-array.

In order to do this, though, we have to construct a format on the fly to pack each string in the vector. Suppose we have the string *hello*. Its length is 5, so we need the format *5s*. If the string is *pragmatic*, though, we need *9s*, and so on. The solution is to use the three lines:

```
numChar = len(str)
format = "%ds" % numChar
data = pack(format, str)
```

which replaces the *"%d"* in *"%ds"* with the length of *str*. We then use this customized format to pack the string itself.

Putting these two ideas together, we have

```
def packVec(vec):
    buf = pack("i", len(vec))
    for v in vec:
        buf += pack("i", len(v))
        format = "%ds" % len(v)
        buf += pack(format, v)
    return buf
def unpackVec(buf):
    intSize = calcsize("i")
    num = unpack("i", buf[0:intSize])[0]
    pos = intSize
    result = []
    for i in range(num):
        length = unpack("i", buf[pos:pos+intSize])[0]
        pos += intSize
        format = "%ds" % length
        str = unpack(format, buf[pos:pos+length])[0]
        result.append(str)
        pos += length
    return result
```

Example: Archiving Random Numbers

Everyone in this business has a "weird job" story. Mine is the time I had to come up with an efficient way to store data sets that contained several million integers. I was consulting for a company that did a lot of defense work at the time; they never told me what the integers represented, or who was going to use them, but I did know that

- A typical data set contained 1–2 million values;

- Their order didn't matter; and

- The values obeyed an exponential distribution. On average, 90% were small enough to fit into 8 bits, 9% would fit into 16, 0.9% would fit into 24, and only the remaining 0.1% needed a full 32 bits.

Now, if I store every value as a 32-bit integer, I'll need $4N$ bytes to store the whole data set (since each integer will need 4 bytes). However, if their order doesn't matter, I can sort them so that all the values small enough to fit into 8 bits are together, followed by all the values that need 16 bits, followed by those that need more than 16 bits. (I decided to handle the 24-bit and 32-bit values together, since Python doesn't have a packing format for 24-bit integers.) I can then store the 8-bit values in one byte each, the 16-bit values in 2 bytes, and the larger values in 4 bytes.

Statistically, this scheme will use $0.9N+0.18N+0.04N$, or $1.12N$, bytes. Oh, but I'll also need to store a header telling me how many values of each kind I actually have; otherwise, I won't know how many of each kind to unpack. If I use three 32-bit integers for the counts, my total storage requirements are $12+1.12N$ bytes. A little math shows that this is more efficient as soon as there are more than five values; when there's a million values, it uses only 28% as much storage as the naive scheme would. That might not seem to matter much, given how cheap disk space is, but with hundreds of sets, each of which had to be moved over a 56K dial-up line (yeah, it was a while ago), the compression was worthwhile.

Here's the routine that does the packing:

```
FMT_HDR = "3i"
LEN_HDR = struct.calcsize(FMT_HDR)
FMT_08 = "B"
FMT_16 = "h"
FMT_32 = "i"
def save(data):
    data.sort()
    num08 = bisect.bisect_left(data, 0x01 << 8)
    num16 = bisect.bisect_left(data, 0x01 << 16)
    num32 = len(data)
    result = cStringIO.StringIO()
    result.write(struct.pack(FMT_HDR, num08, num16, num32))
    i = 0
    while i < num08:
        result.write(struct.pack(FMT_08, data[i] & 0xFF))
        i += 1
    while i < num16:
        result.write(struct.pack(FMT_16, data[i] & 0xFFFF))
        i += 1
    while i < num32:
        result.write(struct.pack(FMT_32, data[i]))
        i += 1
    return result.getvalue()
```

bisect.bisect_left() just does a binary search on sorted data to find where a particular value would go. The two values I use as pivots are the smallest that *won't* fit into 8 bits and the smallest that won't fit into 16. Their indices tell me where the top of the 8-bit and 16-bit value ranges lie.

The rest of this function is pretty straightforward. Once I know how many 8-bit values there are, I pack them one by one into a buffer, using a single byte of storage for each. I then repeat the process for the 16-bit values and then do it once more for everything that's left. Note that I'm appending to a *StringIO*, rather than to a string. If I did the latter, Python would allocate an entirely new string for each append, which would be terribly slow. (Java behaves the same way: strings are immutable, so *"abc"+"def"+"ghi"* actually allocates a new string to hold *"abc"+"def"*, copies six characters into it, then allocates another new string to hold the final result and copies *"abcdef"* and *"ghi"* into it.)

Unpacking is almost as simple—almost, because it's important to remember the difference between the index of the item being unpacked and the index of its location in the buffer:

```
def load(buffer):
    result = []
    num08, num16, num32 = struct.unpack(FMT_HDR, buffer[0:LEN_HDR])
    loc = LEN_HDR
    num = 0
    while num < num08:
        result.append(struct.unpack(FMT_08, buffer[loc])[0])
        loc += 1
        num += 1
    while num < num16:
        result.append(struct.unpack(FMT_16, buffer[loc:loc+2])[0])
        loc += 2
        num += 1
    while num < num32:
        result.append(struct.unpack(FMT_32, buffer[loc:loc+4])[0])
        loc += 4
        num += 1
    return result
```

As always, the job's not done until there's a few simple tests in the file as well:

```
if __name__ == "__main__":
    tests = [
        [],
        [0x00000003],
        [0x00000003, 0x00000007, 0x00000009],
        [0x00000123],
        [0x00000003, 0x00000123],
        [0x00000123, 0x00000003],
        [0x00011111],
        [0x00000003, 0x00000123, 0x00000003, 0x00011111]
    ]
    for t in tests:
        packed = save(t)
        unpacked = load(packed)
        t.sort()
        assert t == unpacked
```

Here, I've written the test data in hex so that it's easier for me to see how many bits each value requires.

The moral of this story is that even when you're "just" crunching data, a few back-of-the-envelope calculations can save you (and your customers) a lot of grief. This variable-length storage scheme is harder to understand than a brute-force approach, but reducing the data transmission time from just under four minutes to just over one made it worthwhile.

Variable Counts

Data that describes other data, like the lengths stored above, is called *metadata*.   *metadata* By using metadata more aggressively, we can store arbitrary structures in a way that will allow anyone to unpack them. The trick is to store format specifiers themselves in the packed data so that whoever has to unpack it can ask the data what it contains.

For example, suppose we want to back up the tables in a database. The records in one table contain two strings and a pair of integers; the records in another contain a single string, four floating-point numbers, and an 8-bit security code, and so on. We don't want to have to build (and maintain) separate packing and unpacking functions for each table, so instead, we'll build one packing function that stores the following:

- a 4-byte integer N that records the length of the metadata;
- an N-byte format descriptor that describes the layout of each record; and
- the records themselves, each of which is in the format described by the metadata.

Making data blocks self-describing in this way has two advantages. First, as mentioned, one pair of pack and unpack functions can handle arbitrary record sets; we don't need to write separate ones for each different data format. Second, and perhaps more important, if the data carries its own format information around, there's no way that format information can get lost. Few things are as frustrating as having the data you need on your hard drive but not being able to read it....

Using metadata has some disadvantages as well, of course. One is that a general unpacking function is slower than one that is tailored for a particular data format. This reflects the second disadvantage: generalized packing and unpacking functions are more complicated to write than specialized ones. However, they are still simpler than the sum of all the specialized functions we would otherwise have to write.

The packing function is simpler than you might expect:

```python
def metaPack(format, data):
    # Length of metadata.
    result = pack("i", len(format))

    # Metadata.
    tmp = "%ds" % len(format)
    result += pack(tmp, format)

    # Records.
    for d in data:
        d = [format] + d
        result += pack(*d)

    # Done.
    return result
```

Note that the expression pack(*d) means, "Call the method pack() with the values in the list *d* as arguments."

After everything else we've seen, unpacking isn't too bad either:

```python
def metaUnpack(data):
    # Length of metadata.
    intSize = calcsize("i")
    formatLen = unpack("i", data[0:intSize])[0]

    # Metadata.
    tmp = "%ds" % formatLen
    format = unpack(tmp, data[intSize:intSize+formatLen])[0]
    recordSize = calcsize(format)
    pos = intSize + formatLen

    # Records.
    result = []
    while pos < len(data):
        tmp = data[pos:pos+recordSize]
        d = unpack(format, tmp)
        result.append(list(d))
        pos += recordSize

    # Done.
    return result
```

Lost Data?

There's a persistent bit of folklore to the effect that the U.S. National Archives has "lost" the data from the 1960 Census. According to the story, the census data is on obsolete computer tapes that can no longer be read by today's machines.

In fact, everything was copied onto modern media long ago, and is regularly used by scholars and statisticians.

But because census data must be kept private until seventy-two years after its collection, the rumor will probably persist until the data is made public in 2032.

See `http://archives.gov/publications/prologue/winter_2000_1960_census.html` for more details.

Finally, here are some tests:

```python
if __name__ == "__main__":
    tests = [
        ["i",   [[1]]],
        ["i",   [[1], [2]]],

        ["3s",  [["xyz"]]],
        ["3s",  [["abc"], ["def"]]],

        ["f3s", [[1.0, "pqr"]]],
        ["f3s", [[2.0, "stu"], [3.0, "vwx"]]]
    ]
    for (format, original) in tests:
        tmp = metaPack(format, original)
        print repr(tmp)
        dup = metaUnpack(tmp)
        assert dup == original
```

Let's take a closer look at the last of these tests. The format string *f3s* tells pack() that each record is a float and a three-character string. Our packed data is therefore

- a 4-byte representation of the number 3 (since the format string is three characters long),
- a three-character format string, and
- two seven-byte records.

5.4 Summary

Joel Spolsky's Law of Leaky Abstractions[5] says that "All non-trivial abstractions, to some degree, are leaky." What that means is that the layers of software we build to insulate ourselves from the details of what processor we're using, or how bytes get from disk to network to screen and back, are never perfect; sooner or later, something goes wrong at a higher level that can be explained and fixed only at a lower one.

This is never truer than when you're working with binary data. The order of bytes in an integer, the way strings are stored, how parameters are passed, and even such simple things as adding two numbers are all suddenly things that you have to pay attention to. Here are a few rules from this chapter to help you:

- Binary formats are useful when text or XML would be too fat or too slow. Using them isn't free, though, since generic tools usually can't handle binary files. Think *very* carefully before creating a new binary format; when you're processing binary data, *always* look for off-the-shelf libraries before writing your own.

- Computers don't store numbers; they store bits. Overflow, bit shifting, and unpacking data with the wrong format can shatter the illusion in a nanosecond.

- Data outlives the software that created it, the hardware it was created on, operating systems, storage media, and even countries. (Just ask genealogists trying to decipher electronic birth certificates from the former Soviet Union.) Documenting your data formats is essential, but it's just as essential to make sure that whatever documentation you write can't be misplaced. The best way to do this is to store the format as part of the data itself.

---

[5]http://www.joelonsoftware.com/articles/LeakyAbstractions.html

## Chapter 6

Relational Databases

Text, XML, images...They're all important, but most of the data people really care about lives in relational databases. Commercial systems like Oracle have dominated corporate IT since the 1980s, but open source alternatives like MySQL,[1] PostgreSQL[2] and SQLite[3] are now at the heart of millions of web sites and small companies around the world.

Relational databases store data in *tables*. Each table is organized into *columns* and *rows*; each column stores just one type of data (such as integer, string, or Boolean), while each row is a single data record.

tables
columns
rows

Every sensible database table has a *primary key*, which may include the values from one or more columns.[4] Just as in a dictionary, each primary key must be unique: no two rows in a particular table can be keyed by the same values.

primary key

Relational databases are accessed using a specialized language called SQL (which originally stood for Structured Query Language). which provides some very powerful ways to search and combine data. In this chapter, you'll meet the 10% of SQL that accounts for 90% of common use and see how to query databases from languages like Java and Python.

As a running example, I'll use a database that keeps track of who's doing what in a small consulting company (Figure 6.1 on page 139). This database contains four tables: Person, which stores information about employees; Customer, which stores information about who's paying for projects; Project, which lists all the projects; and Assigned, which records who's working on what. The highlighted columns for

---

[1] http://www.mysql.org
[2] http://www.postgresql.org
[3] http://www.sqlite.org
[4] I'm simplifying a lot here—you can create databases in which some tables don't have primary keys—but it's close enough to the truth that I'm willing to relegate the disclaimer to a footnote.

each table make up its key; Figure 6.2 on page 140 shows the actual data in each table.

6.1 Simple Queries

It's 9:15 on Monday morning, and the boss wants a list of employees' names to put on a seating plan. To get them, we need to know which table to examine, and which columns to get from it. The answer to the first is Person; the answer to the second, FirstName and LastName. In SQL, we can write this query down almost exactly as we would say it:

```
-- Get employees' forenames and surnames.
SELECT Person.FirstName, Person.LastName FROM Person;
```

Depending on which database system you use, the output will look something like

Dave	Thomas
Andy	Hunt
Greg	Wilson
Grace	Hopper
Alan	Turing
Chuck	Babbage

As you can see, SQL's syntax is pretty simple. Unlike most languages, it is case-insensitive: *from*, *FROM*, and *fRoM* all mean the same thing. By convention, though, most people write keywords in UPPER CASE and the names of tables and fields in Title Case or CamelCase.

Similarly, while you're allowed to write a field name like FirstName on its own when there's no danger of ambiguity, it's good style to always qualify it with the table name, as in *Person.FirstName*.

Finally, statements can span multiple lines and should end in a semicolon;[5] comments start with a double dash and extend to the end of the line.

We can sort the list alphabetically by surname like this:

```
-- All consultants, sorted by surname.
SELECT    Person.LastName, Person.FirstName
FROM      Person
ORDER BY Person.LastName ASC;
```

ORDER BY rearranges rows according to the values in a particular column; *ASC* puts them into ascending order, while *DESC* puts them into descending (reverse) order.

---

[5]Many SQL implementations don't require the semicolon, but it never hurts to put it in.

Person

Empid	integer	Employee ID
FirstName	string	Person's first name
LastName	string	Person's last name
Rate	decimal	Charge-out rate per day

Assigned

Empid	integer	ID of employee assigned to project
Projid	integer	Project employee is assigned to
CustId	integer	Customer ID
StartDate	date	When work starts (or started)
EndDate	date	When work ends (or is supposed to)

Customer

Custid	integer	Customer ID
ContactInfo	string	Customer contact information

Project

Projid	integer	Project ID
ProjName	string	Project name
CustId	integer	Customer ID
StartDate	date	When project starts
EndDate	date	When project should end

Figure 6.1: EXAMPLE TABLES

Person	3001	Dave	Thomas	400	
	3002	Andy	Hunt	400	
	4001	Greg	Wilson	320	
	4002	Grace	Hopper	500	
	4003	Alan	Turing	500	
	4004	Chuck	Babbage	125	

Project	904	RubyMath	70043	2004-05-01	2004-10-30
	905	DbBridge	70047	2004-05-01	2004-10-30

Customer	70043	MegaCorp Inc.
	70047	Deadlines 'R' Us
	70101	University of Euphoria

Assigned	3001	904	2005-02-01	2005-02-28
	3002	904	2005-02-01	2005-03-15
	4001	904	2005-02-01	2005-03-31
	4001	905	2005-01-10	2005-02-22
	4002	905	2005-01-20	2005-04-01
	4004	905	2005-02-10	2005-03-31

Figure 6.2: Example Values

This query's output is

Babbage	Chuck
Hopper	Grace
Hunt	Andy
Thomas	Dave
Turing	Alan
Wilson	Greg

Joins

It's 9:45 a.m., and the question is, "Who's paying for the RubyMath project?" The information we want is divided between two tables: the project's name is in Project, but the customer's name is in Customer. The two tables are connected by the values in the CustId column, so what we have to do is *join* the tables on those values. Here's the SQL:

```
-- Get name of company paying for RubyMath project.
SELECT Customer.ContactInfo
FROM   Customer, Project
WHERE (Customer.CustId = Project.CustId)
  AND (Project.ProjName = "RubyMath");
```

and here's its output:

Eating My Own Cooking

I used SQLite to create the examples for this chapter. When run from the command line, its output actually looks like this:

```
70043|MegaCorp Inc.
70047|Deadlines 'R' Us
70101|University of Euphoria
```

What I want is more like this:

```
<?xml version="1.0" encoding="UTF-8"?>
<!DOCTYPE chapter SYSTEM "../../local/xml/markup.dtd">

<smalltable colspec="l l">
<row>
  <col><p>70043</p></col>
  <col><p>MegaCorp Inc.</p></col>
</row>
<row>
  <col><p>70047</p></col>
  <col><p>Deadlines 'R' Us</p></col>
</row>
<row>
  <col><p>70101</p></col>
  <col><p>University of Euphoria</p></col>
</row>
</smalltable>
```

No problem: all I have to do is write a little Python script to read in lines, split them on vertical bars, and print the fields with appropriate tags wrapped around them. Oh, and since there are a lot of examples, I should write a Makefile that re-creates each table, just in case I change the data in the database (which I did twice while writing this chapter) or the format that I want (four times).

MegaCorp Inc.

Let's take a closer look at that SQL, since most of the queries you'll ever write will have a similar structure. When a database evaluates a query, it always behaves as if it had done the following (Figure 6.3 on page 143):

1. Construct the *cross product* of the tables in the *FROM* clause.

2. Evaluate the condition in the *WHERE* clause once for each row in that cross product, keeping only those rows that satisfy it.

3. Keep the values in the columns specified in the *SELECT* portion of the query.

So what's a cross product? It's just all possible combinations of elements from two (or more) sets. For example, the cross product of {a,b} and {c,d} is the

> ### ⌣ Joe Asks...
> #### Is SQL a Standard?
> ───
>
> In theory, yes, SQL is an international standard, defined by the American National Standards Institute (a U.S. government body) and the International Organization for Standardization (ISO). The language was originally defined in 1986/87, then expanded in 1992 to create SQL-92, and expanded again seven years later to create SQL-99.
>
> In practice, most databases provide all of the original spec but only a subset of SQL-92; only a few implement the extra features defined by SQL-99. Instead, almost every database provides its own idiosyncratic way (or ways) to do things. This is one of the reasons that the object/relational mapping tools discussed in Section 6.5, *Objects and Tables*, on page 164 have become so popular: they do their best to hide the differences between different databases so that programmers don't have to write five slight variations on every query their program needs.

four pairs {a,c}, {a,d}, {b,c}, and {b,d}. Similarly, the cross product of the database tables Person and Project is

70043	MegaCorp Inc.	904	RubyMath	70043	2004-05-01	2004-10-30
70043	MegaCorp Inc.	905	DbBridge	70047	2004-05-01	2004-10-30
70047	Deadlines 'R' Us	904	RubyMath	70043	2004-05-01	2004-10-30
70047	Deadlines 'R' Us	905	DbBridge	70047	2004-05-01	2004-10-30
70101	University of Euphoria	904	RubyMath	70043	2004-05-01	2004-10-30
70101	University of Euphoria	905	DbBridge	70047	2004-05-01	2004-10-30

Each row of the Person table is combined with each row of the Project table to create a row of the result, which contains all the columns from both of the original tables. Since there are three rows in Customer, and two in Project, the cross product has six rows. Similarly, since there are two columns in Customer and five in Project, the output has seven columns.

In principle, therefore, the database creates a 6×9 table, then examines its rows to find those where

- the project name is *RubyMath*; and

- the value in the Customer.CustID column matches the value in the Project.CustID column.

In practice, of course, the database isn't nearly this inefficient. For example, since *RubyMath* is a constant, the database actually starts by selecting the row from

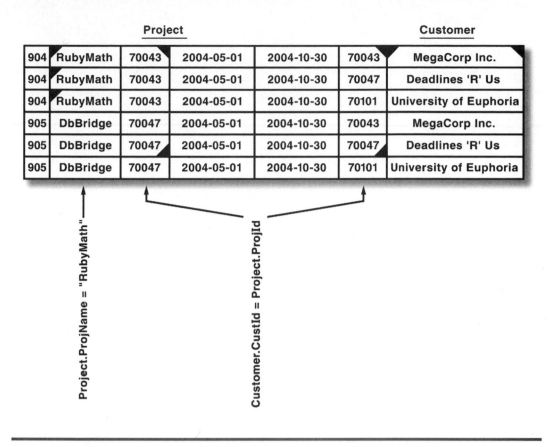

Figure 6.3: CROSS-PRODUCT AND JOIN

Project with that name. It then finds rows in Customer whose customer IDs match those of the rows already taken from Project and selects the ContactInfo values. All of this happens behind the programmer's back—different databases may use different optimization algorithms (which is why they have different prices), but all behave *as if* they were doing things the naive, inefficient way.

Let's use a join to get the names of the employees working on the RubyMath project. The information we want is divided between three tables: the IDs of the employees working on the project are in the Assigned table, their names are in Person, and the name of the project itself is in Project. Here goes:

```
-- Get forenames and surnames of employees on RubyMath project.
SELECT Person.FirstName, Person.LastName
FROM   Person, Project, Assigned
WHERE (Person.EmpId = Assigned.EmpId)
  AND (Project.ProjName = "RubyMath")
  AND (Assigned.ProjId = Project.ProjId);
```

Its output is

Dave   Thomas
Andy   Hunt
Greg   Wilson

Finding Overlaps

It's 10:17 a.m., and the company lawyer who has been working on intellectual property issues wants to know if anyone is assigned to both the RubyMath and DbBridge projects. Our first attempt at a query looks like this:

```
-- Wrong way to ask whether someone is assigned to two projects.
SELECT Assigned.EmpId
FROM    Assigned
WHERE (Assigned.ProjId = 904)
  AND (Assigned.ProjId = 905);
```

This query finds no matches, even though employee 4001 (yours truly) is actually supposed to be working on both projects. What's going wrong?

The answer is that our query would work only if Assigned.ProjId could take on two values at once, which it can't. Like a variable in a program, the Assigned.ProjId value in each row of the cross product can store only a single value. If that value is 904, it can't be 905, and vice versa, which means that the *WHERE* clause can never be satisfied.

All right, if *AND* won't work, what about *OR*? If we change the query to

```
-- Wrong way to ask whether someone is assigned to two projects.
SELECT Assigned.EmpId
FROM    Assigned
WHERE (Assigned.ProjId = 904)
   OR (Assigned.ProjId = 905);
```

we get

3001
3002
4001
4001
4002
4004

Uh, what? Why does the output include every single employee ID? And why does 4001 appear twice? Well, go back to the evaluation rules. To evaluate this query, the database constructs the cross product of Assigned with itself. Since Assigned has six rows, the result has thirty-six. Every one of those has either 904 or 905 as the project ID, which means that every row satisfies the query's *WHERE* condition.

Modern Joins

Modern dialects of SQL offer several different ways to join database tables. For example, the ideologically correct way to write our earlier query is

```
SELECT  Customer.ContactInfo
FROM    Customer INNER JOIN Project
ON      Customer.CustId = Project.CustId
WHERE   Project.ProjName = "RubyMath";
```

(Feh03) describes the differences between inner joins, left joins, right joins, and outer joins and explains when you should use each.

The result is that each employee ID is printed out once for each row of Assigned, which definitely isn't what we wanted.

The trick is to join Assigned with itself so that we have two project IDs in hand at one time.[6] To do this, we have to create a temporary *alias* for the table. Suppose we have a simple table called Stuff that looks like this:

Left	Right
A	B
C	D

If we execute

```
SELECT * FROM Stuff First, Stuff Second;
```

then the database creates two temporary copies of the Stuff table called First and Second, which it can then join with each other to create

First.Left	First.Right	Second.Left	Second.Right
A	B	A	B
A	B	C	D
C	D	A	B
C	D	C	D

Note the use of * in the *SELECT*. As you can probably guess, it means, "Give me all the data." Note also that no database worth installing would actually duplicate Stuff. Instead, it would look at what your query was doing with the temporary tables and optimize them away. The end effect is the same: our query can now compare different rows of a single table against one another.

---

[6]We can also solve this problem with subqueries, which we'll meet in Section 6.2, *Nesting and Negation*, on page 147.

Aliases in hand, let's go back and find out who has been assigned to both project 904 and project 905:

```
-- Right way to ask whether someone is assigned to projects 904 and 905.
SELECT A.EmpId
FROM    Assigned A, Assigned B
WHERE (A.EmpId = B.EmpId)
   AND (A.ProjId = 904)
   AND (B.ProjId = 905);
```

This query does the following:

1. (Pretends to) duplicate the Assigned table to create two temporary tables called A and B.
2. Joins the rows of the two tables on the employee ID so that each row gives information about a pair of project assignments for a single employee.
3. Looks for rows where the first project ID is 904 and the second is 905.
4. Keeps the employee ID from those rows.

The output is a satisfying

4001

All right; if we want to find anyone who's assigned to any two projects, not just 904 and 905, we can do this:

```
-- Wrong way to ask whether someone is assigned to any two projects.
SELECT A.EmpId
FROM    Assigned A, Assigned B
WHERE (A.EmpId = B.EmpId)
   AND (A.ProjId != B.ProjId);
```

Right? Wrong. The query above produces

4001
4001

Why the double counting? Well, when the database joins Assigned with itself, it produces one row in which A.ProjId is 904 and B.ProjId is 905, and another in which A.ProjId is 905 and B.ProjId is 904. We can hack around this by using the fact that project IDs are integers and keep only those rows where A's entry is less than B's:

```
-- Right way to ask whether someone is assigned to two projects.
SELECT A.EmpId
FROM    Assigned A, Assigned B
WHERE (A.EmpId = B.EmpId)
   AND (A.ProjId < B.ProjId);
```

Using < instead of != ensures that we count each pair of project IDs only once. Another solution is to let the database sort it out for us like this:

```
-- Right way to ask whether someone is assigned to two projects.
SELECT DISTINCT A.EmpId
FROM    Assigned A, Assigned B
```

```
WHERE (A.EmpId = B.EmpId)
  AND (A.ProjId != B.ProjId);
```

The keyword *DISTINCT* means exactly what you think: it tells the database to throw away redundant rows of output.

6.2 Nesting and Negation

The little bit of SQL you've seen so far will probably let you write 90% of the queries you'll ever need. Well, maybe 80%—there's still one big idea that needs to be introduced, and that's how to do *negation*.

Suppose the company lawyer wants a list of everyone who *isn't* assigned to Ruby-Math (project 904)—in other words, everyone who can be put to work for one of MegaCorp Inc.'s competitors without (much) risk of a lawsuit. We can't just select rows from the assignment table where ProjId is not 904, because that would include employee 4001 (that's me), but I'm assigned to both RubyMath and other projects.

It turns out that no amount of clever table joining will solve this problem either, at least not in the general case. What we need to do is

1. Select every row we *don't* want.

2. Subtract them from the set of all rows.

In other words, the set of rows we want is the set of all rows minus the set of rows we don't want. This is a little roundabout, but once you get used to it, it... well, OK, it still seems a little roundabout.

First, we need to learn how to nest one query in another so that we can select the rows we want to subtract from the total. Take a look at the following query:

```
-- Select people who are assigned to the RubyMath project.
SELECT Person.FirstName, Person.LastName
FROM   Person
WHERE  Person.EmpId IN
       (SELECT Assigned.EmpId
        FROM   Assigned
        WHERE (Assigned.ProjId = 904));
```

When the database manager evaluates this query, it runs the *subquery* first to find the employee IDs of everyone who's assigned to project 904. It then matches those values against the ones stored in the Person table to select people's first and last names. Figure 6.4 on the next page shows the evaluation process; the output is the three lines:

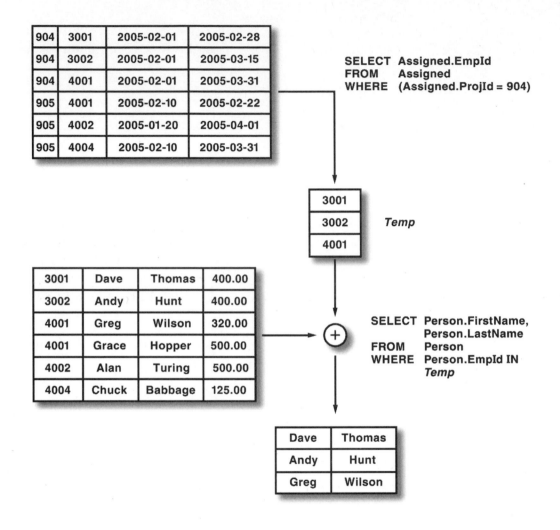

Figure 6.4: EVALUATION PROCESS

Dave   Thomas
Andy   Hunt
Greg   Wilson

Now, let's add one word to the query: *NOT*. If we tell the outer query to keep people who are *not* in the set created by the subquery, we should have all the employees who *aren't* assigned to project 904:

```
-- Select people who are NOT assigned to the RubyMath project.
SELECT  Person.FirstName, Person.LastName
FROM    Person
WHERE   Person.EmpId NOT IN
        (SELECT Assigned.EmpId
         FROM   Assigned
         WHERE (Assigned.ProjId = 904));
```

Sure enough, the output is

Grace	Hopper
Alan	Turing
Chuck	Babbage

We could also move the *NOT* outside the nested query:

```
-- Select people who are NOT assigned to the RubyMath project.
SELECT  Person.FirstName, Person.LastName
FROM    Person
WHERE   NOT Person.EmpId IN
        (SELECT Assigned.EmpId
         FROM   Assigned
         WHERE (Assigned.ProjId = 904));
```

Which form you use is up to you.

Before moving on, let's clean this query up a bit. Magic numbers are always a bad idea in programs, and 904 is definitely a magic number. So, rather than asking who's not assigned to a project by number, let's ask who's not assigned to it by name:

```
-- Select people who are NOT assigned to the RubyMath project.
SELECT  Person.FirstName, Person.LastName
FROM    Person
WHERE   Person.EmpId NOT IN
        (SELECT Assigned.EmpId
         FROM   Assigned, Project
         WHERE (Assigned.ProjId = Project.ProjId)
         AND   (Project.ProjName = "RubyMath"));
```

As you can see, a subquery can include everything any other query can include. In fact, queries can be nested several layers deep (although most database systems put an upper limit on nesting). Whenever you see a deeply nested query, you should always read it from the bottom up: figure out what the most deeply nested subquery returns, then look at how the enclosing query filters its values, and so on. It's just like reading a Unix pipe from left to right.

Other Uses for Nested Queries

Nested queries and sideways thinking about sets can be combined to answer many other questions about the data in a database. For example, suppose we want to find people who are assigned to exactly one project. We can do this right now using the trick from Section 6.1, *Finding Overlaps*, on page 144: join Assigned to itself so that we can compare project IDs to find people doing two (or more) projects and then subtract them from the set of all people:

```
-- Select people who are assigned to exactly one project.
SELECT Person.FirstName, Person.LastName
FROM   Person, Assigned
WHERE (Person.EmpId = Assigned.EmpId)
  AND (Assigned.EmpId NOT IN
        (SELECT A.EmpId
         FROM   Assigned A, Assigned B
         WHERE (A.EmpId = B.EmpId)
           AND (A.ProjId < B.ProjId)));
```

The output is

Dave	Thomas
Andy	Hunt
Grace	Hopper
Chuck	Babbage

It's clumsy, but it works. Counting how many projects each person is assigned to is cleaner; we'll see how in Section 6.3, *Aggregation and Views*, on the next page.

All right, let's try another query: who is assigned to either project 904 or project 905 but not both? Since these are the only two projects in the sample database, the answer ought to be the same as the answer to the previous query. If there were more projects, though, the previous query would include people assigned to them; we want a query that is project-specific.

Here are the steps:

1. Find everyone who is assigned to either project.
2. Subtract the people who are assigned to both.

The query is

```
-- Find people in 904 or 905, but not both.
SELECT Person.FirstName, Person.LastName
FROM   Person, Assigned
WHERE (Person.EmpId = Assigned.EmpId)
  AND ((Assigned.ProjId = 904) OR (Assigned.ProjId = 905))
  AND (Assigned.ProjId NOT IN
        (SELECT A.ProjId
         FROM   Assigned A, Assigned B
         WHERE (A.ProjId = 904) AND (B.ProjId = 905)));
```

and the output is

Greg	Wilson
Grace	Hopper
Chuck	Babbage

(Yes, I should be using projects' names, rather than their IDs...I'm a bad person sometimes.)

Finally, we can use nested queries to find maximum or minimum values. Once again, the trick is to find all the values that aren't the maximum or minimum and subtract them from the set of all values.

It's 1:47 p.m. We've just landed a contract with a major software developer located in the Pacific Northwest and want to assign the most expensive contractors we have. We need to find people such that no one else has a higher charge-out rate. We do this by joining Person with itself and comparing each pair's rate. If for a person A, there's a person B with a higher rate, we keep person A in the set. We then subtract this set (people who aren't the most expensive) from the set of all people:

```
-- Find the most expensive contractors.
SELECT Person.FirstName, Person.LastName
FROM    Person
WHERE (Person.Rate NOT IN
       (SELECT A.Rate
        FROM   Person A, Person B
        WHERE  A.Rate < B.Rate));
```

The result is

Grace   Hopper
Alan   Turing

This kind of double negation can be pretty mind-bending, even for experienced developers. When you have to write queries like this, it's always best to build them from the bottom up, one step at a time. Run each query and check its output to make sure it's generating what you expect and then wrap another one around it, until you have the data you actually want.

6.3   Aggregation and Views

Good news: in response to our pricing, that Pacific Northwest software company has come back and asked, "What's the average rate for your consultants?" Hmm...as well as selecting values, we now have to combine them. How can we do that?

Use SQL's built-in functions. Take a look at the following query:

```
-- Get the average rate for all consultants.
SELECT AVG(Person.Rate)
FROM    Person;
```

The AVG() function combines, or *aggregates*, all the values in a column to produce a single row, so this query's output is simply:

374.166666666667

Similar functions like MAX() and MIN() can (and should) be used in place of the negate-and-subtract technique shown in Section 6.2, *Other Uses for Nested Queries*, on page 149: they're easier to read, and will run faster on most systems.

What about finding the total hourly rate for each project in the database? The total part is easy: there's a built-in function called SUM(). But we want to sum each project separately, so we somehow have to group the rows for each project.

GROUP BY to the rescue. As the name suggests, this creates groups of rows having equal values in one or more columns; aggregation functions like SUM() then work on each group independently. This means that the result has as many rows as there were distinct values in the input.

Let's take a closer look. To get one row for each person working on a project, with the project's name and the person's rate, we can run

```
-- Get the average rate for all consultants.
SELECT    Project.ProjName, Person.Rate
FROM      Person, Assigned, Project
WHERE     (Person.EmpId = Assigned.EmpId)
AND       (Project.ProjId = Assigned.ProjId);
```

which produces

RubyMath	400
RubyMath	400
RubyMath	320
DbBridge	320
DbBridge	500
DbBridge	125

If we group rows according to project and calculate a sum, the query is

```
-- Get the average rate for all consultants.
SELECT    Project.ProjName, SUM(Person.Rate)
FROM      Person, Assigned, Project
WHERE     (Person.EmpId = Assigned.EmpId)
AND       (Project.ProjId = Assigned.ProjId)
GROUP BY Assigned.ProjId;
```

The output is

RubyMath	1120
DbBridge	945

What if we want to find the consultants on each project who cost less than the average for that project? This is getting pretty involved, but queries like this come up all the time in the real world: companies want to know who the top 10% of their customers are by sales, for example, or which of their salespeople have sold less than average in the last quarter.

As is usually the case in programming, the right way to tackle this problem is to break it into smaller problems and solve each in turn. What we want is a table with two columns: the project ID and the average rate for the consultants working on that project. If we had that, it would be straightforward to join it with Person to get the information we want.

SQL's *views* do exactly what we want. A view is basically a stored *SELECT* statement whose result can be treated like a temporary table. When a view's name is used where a table's name would be, the corresponding *SELECT* is evaluated and the results fed to the outer query. Industrial-strength databases cache the results of evaluating views, so if the underlying tables haven't changed, nothing is actually recalculated when a view is reused. *views*

Here's how to create the view we want:

```
CREATE VIEW ProjAveRate AS
   SELECT    Project.ProjId AS ProjId,
             AVG(Person.Rate) AS AveRate
   FROM      Person, Assigned, Project
   WHERE     (Person.EmpId = Assigned.EmpId)
   AND       (Project.ProjId = Assigned.ProjId)
   GROUP BY Assigned.ProjId;
```

The view's name is ProjAveRate; it has two columns called ProjId and AveRate. Once it has been defined, we can use it as if it were just another table, like this:

```
SELECT ProjAveRate.ProjId, Person.FirstName, Person.LastName,
       Person.Rate, ProjAveRate.AveRate
FROM   Person, Assigned, ProjAveRate
WHERE (Person.EmpId = Assigned.EmpId)
  AND (Assigned.ProjId = ProjAveRate.ProjId)
  AND (Person.Rate > ProjAveRate.AveRate);
```

This matches people with the projects they're assigned to and then compares their rate to the average rate for that project. When we run it, we get

904	Dave	Thomas	400	373.333333333333
904	Andy	Hunt	400	373.333333333333
905	Greg	Wilson	320	315
905	Grace	Hopper	500	315

As a quick sanity check, we can change the > to a < and run it again. As it should be, the output is all the people who weren't in the first list:

904	Greg	Wilson	320	373.333333333333
905	Chuck	Babbage	125	315

Nulls

In the real world, data is never complete: there are always people who don't have a fax number or whose blood type is unknown. The wrong way to represent this in a database is to use a dummy value, such as 000-0000 or *UNKNOWN*. The right way is to use *NULL*.[7]

Like *null*, *None*, and its other counterparts, SQL's *NULL* means, "There's no value here." It is *not* the same as zero, the empty string, or any other value—it doesn't have a data type. Most important, *NULL* isn't equal to anything, not even to itself (although *DISTINCT* does group all *NULL* values together). Instead, you must check to see whether a value is *NULL* by using *IS NULL*.

Since *NULL* doesn't have a value, any computation involving *NULL* returns *NULL* as its result.[8] This means that SQL actually uses *three-valued logic*, where the three values are true, false, and "I don't know." For example, *True AND NULL* is *NULL*, but so is *False AND NULL*.

What does this mean for data crunching? Well, the first thing is to find out whether any of the tables you're working with can contain *NULL*. You can do this by looking at the table definitions (discussed in Section 6.4, *Creating and Deleting Tables*, on the next page) or by running a query:

```
SELECT *
FROM    Person
WHERE (Person.EmpId IS NULL)
   OR (Person.FirstName IS NULL)
   OR (Person.LastName IS NULL)
   OR (Person.Rate IS NULL);
```

If any of the values you care about are (or could be) *NULL*, you may have to rewrite some of your queries. Remember, *NULL* is not equal to anything, so if you have a query like this:

```
SELECT *
FROM    Project
WHERE   CustId <> 1027;
```

it will select projects whose customer ID is *NULL*. If that isn't what you want, change the query to

```
SELECT *
FROM    Project
WHERE (CustId <> 1027)
  AND (CustId IS NOT NULL);
```

---

[7]Actually, about half of the database world thinks *NULL* is the right way to represent "not applicable"; the other half thinks it should be reserved strictly for "value unknown." This is another of those religious wars that programmers spend their time on in between episodes of *Buffy the Vampire Slayer*.

[8]Well, it's supposed to do this. In practice, *False AND NULL* produces *False* in many databases, while *True OR NULL* produces *True*. Aren't standards wonderful?

6.4   Creating, Updating, and Deleting

After *WTF*, the most commonly used acronym in the database world is *CRUD*, which stands for Create, Read, Update, and Delete. We've seen how to read; it's now time to look at how to create tables, update them, and delete information we (hope we) no longer need.

Schemas and Data Types

The definitions of a database's tables are called its *schema*. This includes more than just what types each table's columns have; it also defines the relationships between the tables, such as whether the values in column A of table B correspond to those in column C of table D. Literally hundreds of books discuss how to design a database schema (my favorite is [Her03]). When you're crunching data, though, you will almost always have inherited a schema from someone else; "all" you have to do is figure out what it means.

schema

The data types supported by different databases vary widely: some databases now recognize XML as a special type, for example, while others treat it as text. You can almost always rely on the basic ones shown in Figure 6.5 on the following page, but you should check the documentation for the database you're actually using to be sure.

Creating and Deleting Tables

Creating a table is pretty simple: all we have to do is specify its name, the names and types of its fields, and whether those fields can be null. For example, I created the Person table in the consulting database like this:

```
CREATE TABLE Person(
     EmpId          INTEGER      NOT NULL       PRIMARY KEY,
     FirstName      TEXT         NOT NULL,
     LastName       TEXT         NOT NULL,
     Rate           DECIMAL      NOT NULL
);
```

Notice how I've specified that the employee ID is the table's primary key. You can also specify that some columns are *foreign keys*, which means that their values are keys in other tables—see [Feh03] for details.

Deleting tables is just as easy as creating them. In fact, deleting tables is sometimes *too* easy. All you have to type is

```
DROP TABLE Person;
```

Remember: back up early, back up often....

INTEGER   Signed integers. Some databases may allow you to specify a size between 1 and 8 bytes.

DECIMAL   A fixed-point number, i.e., one that has a fixed numbers of digits after the decimal point. Currency values are almost always stored as DECIMAL.

REAL   A floating-point number of the kind used in most programming languages.

TEXT   A string of text. Some databases require you to specify an upper bound on values' lengths; others impose one. (You will still often see the older syntax VARCHAR(80) used to specify an 80-character string.)

BIT   A string of 0s and 1s. As with TEXT, you may have to specify a maximum length.

DATE   A particular day.

TIME   A specific time of day (hours, minutes, seconds, and possibly milliseconds or microseconds as well).

TIMESTAMP A moment in time (i.e., a DATE and a TIME).

BLOB   A Binary Large OBject, i.e., a bunch of bytes whose internal structure is none of the database's concern. BLOBs are used to store multimedia data (such as audio and video), compiled programs, and everything else that doesn't fit into any other type.

NULL   The type of the special value NULL.

Figure 6.5: SQL DATA TYPES

Indexing

An *index* is an auxiliary data structure that helps the database keep track of the values in a particular table. When to create an index, and which columns to include in it, is a complex subject; the trade-offs between the extra memory and disk space required and the speed gained are often hard to predict. In general, though, an index will help when a column's values are frequently searched, sorted, or used in joins. They won't help (and can actually slow things down) when a column can contain only a small number of distinct values (e.g., "male" or "female"), or are rarely used in queries.

You probably won't ever create an index when crunching data, since high performance over the long term isn't your main concern. You usually won't even have to care if the tables you're working on are indexed or not, either, since once an index is created, it does its work silently thereafter. Howevever, if you're crunching millions of records, it's worth getting the database administrator to look over your queries, just in case they're going to bring her system to its knees. (In fact, good DBAs often insist on checking *all* of the SQL being run against "their" database, just as good sys admins insist on checking new packages before users install them.)

Inserting Rows

Every table is empty when first created. To add data to it, you use *INSERT*. In its simplest form, *INSERT* takes the name of the table and the value to be put into each column of the new row:

```
INSERT INTO Person VALUES(3001, "Dave", "Thomas", "400.00");
INSERT INTO Person VALUES(3002, "Andy", "Hunt",   "400.00");
```

Provided you haven't violated any constraints, such as trying to put *NULL* in a column where it isn't allowed, or duplicating a value that is supposed to be unique, the operation adds a new row to the table.

You can also specify values out of order or (if the table permits nulls) leave values out. For example, we can add another couple of consultants to the personnel database name-first like this:

```
INSERT INTO Person(LastName, FirstName, EmpId, Rate)
            VALUES("Turing", "Alan", 4003, "500.00");
INSERT INTO Person(LastName, FirstName, EmpId, Rate)
            VALUES("Babbage", "Chuck", 4004, "125.00");
```

If nothing is provided for a column, the database will automatically insert a null there, unless *NOT NULL* was used in the column's definition. In that case, your database manager will report some kind of error. How comprehensible that error is depends on your database; if you run this:

```
INSERT INTO Person VALUES("Zuse",   "Konrad",   "9000.00");
```

against SQLite, for example, it produces the somewhat misleading

```
INSERT INTO Person VALUES("Zuse",   "Konrad",   "9000.00");
SQL error: no such table: Person
```

You can also insert data from one table directly into another. To create a table with just people's employee IDs and rates, for example, we could use this:

```
CREATE TABLE BriefPerson(
        Id                    INTEGER         NOT NULL,
        Rate                  DECIMAL         NOT NULL
);

INSERT INTO BriefPerson
SELECT        EmpId, Rate
FROM          Person;
```

which would create this:

```
3001    400
3002    400
4001    320
4002    500
4003    500
4004    125
```

Deleting Rows

In order to delete rows, you must identify them using a *SELECT* statement. Everything that matches is erased, so if you are running commands interactively, it is usually—OK, always—a good idea to run the *SELECT* first to make sure that what you're deleting is what you want to delete.

For example, suppose the economic climate has gone a little chilly, and we want to get our most expensive consultants off our books. The following SQL would erase them from the Person table:

```
DELETE  FROM Person
   WHERE Rate > 400.00;
```

Updating Rows

In theory, *INSERT* and *DELETE* are all you need to update values in a database: you just delete the old information and add the new. In practice, it's almost always more efficient to update rows in place, since the database can then reuse memory and disk space instead of allocating and deallocating it.

Normal Forms

Remember the "Don't Repeat Yourself" principle from sidebar 2.2 on page 16? It's even more important when you're working with relational databases. Redundant data makes storage requirements bloat, slows down queries, and makes maintenance a nightmare. (I once worked with a database that stored each user's work phone number in eight places, and their cell number in three. You can imagine what the code to change their address looked like....)

Normalization is the process of removing redundancy and inconsistency from database tables. Depending on how strict you are, the resulting database will be in one of several *normal forms*, each of which builds on its predecessors.

When, why, and how to normalize is out of the scope of this book, but any good introduction to databases, like (Feh03), will explain the following rules in detail:

- First normal form. Each column only contains atomic values, and the table has no repeating groups.

- Second normal form. The primary key is a single column, *or* every non-key value depends on all of the values making up the key.

- Third normal form. No non-key value determines another non-key value.

- Fourth and fifth normal forms. They are kind of hard to explain, but fortunately, they come up so rarely in practice that I've never had to worry about them.

UPDATE to the rescue. Like *DELETE*, *UPDATE* requires you to specify which row or rows you want to change. You must also specify how you want them to change, either by giving new values, or by providing a way to calculate those values.

For example, if we want to increase what we charge for our cheapest consultants, we could execute the following

```
UPDATE  Person
   SET  Rate = Rate * 1.05
 WHERE Rate < 400.00;
```

After this statement runs, the Person table contains

3001	Dave	Thomas	400
3002	Andy	Hunt	400
4001	Greg	Wilson	336
4002	Grace	Hopper	500
4003	Alan	Turing	500
4004	Chuck	Babbage	131.25

Concurrency

Once we start inserting, updating, and deleting rows, we have to worry about what would happen if two or more users tried changing the contents of the database at the same time. We also have to worry about what happens when an operation is interrupted halfway through. I say "when," not "if," because in the modern world, almost all programs interact with databases over a network, and sooner or later, heavy traffic or a careless kick will sever a connection in the middle of a command.

atomic transactions To cope with these situations, relational databases provide *atomic transactions*.[9] A transaction is just one or more operations; atomic means that either all of those operations succeed or no changes are made to the database at all. If several people are using the database at once, the database guarantees that each transaction will appear to have run on its own; in other words, once it has completed all of the transactions, it will look as though they ran in some sequential order, rather than being interleaved.

For example, suppose that every project has to have a team lead. Rather than storing that information in a separate table,[10] we've decided to store a Boolean value to indicate who is presently in charge. When Andy takes over from Dave on Project 909, we have to change this:

| 909 | 3001 | 2005-02-01 | 2005-02-28 | 1 |
| 909 | 3002 | 2005-02-01 | 2005-03-15 | 0 |

to this:

| 909 | 3001 | 2005-02-01 | 2005-02-28 | *0* |
| 909 | 3002 | 2005-02-01 | 2005-03-15 | *1* |

The SQL looks simple:

```
UPDATE    Assigned
   SET    IsLead = 0
```

---

[9]However, the popular open source database MySQL started offering them only a couple of years ago.

[10]This would be a better design, since it wouldn't lead to lots of redundant *False* values in the database.

```
   WHERE (ProjId = 909)
     AND (EmpId = 3001);
UPDATE  Assigned
  SET   IsLead = 1
  WHERE (ProjId = 909)
    AND (EmpId = 3002);
```

If our database server goes down in between the first *UPDATE* and the second, though, the project could be left without a lead. Worse, suppose we had written the statements in the reverse order to set Andy's *IsLead* to 1 and then set Dave's to 0. If the connection dropped, we could wind up with both of them thinking that they were in charge, which, well, I don't know what would happen, but it wouldn't be pretty.

This is where transactions come in. Change the SQL to read

```
BEGIN TRANSACTION;

UPDATE  Assigned
  SET   IsLead = 0
  WHERE (ProjId = 909)
    AND (EmpId = 3001);
UPDATE  Assigned
  SET   IsLead = 1
  WHERE (ProjId = 909)
    AND (EmpId = 3002);

COMMIT TRANSACTION;
```

If statements inside the transaction are interrupted for any reason, the database manager guarantees that there will be no change to the database at all. We could put a hundred inserts, updates, and deletes inside the transaction; either they would all take effect or none of them would.

Transactions also give us the ability to cancel operations once they have started. We can't interrupt individual statements, but if we then change our minds about putting Andy in charge, we could do this:

```
BEGIN TRANSACTION;

UPDATE  Assigned
  SET   IsLead = 0
  WHERE (ProjId = 909)
    AND (EmpId = 3001);
UPDATE  Assigned
  SET   IsLead = 1
  WHERE (ProjId = 909)
    AND (EmpId = 3002);

ROLLBACK TRANSACTION;
```

Rolling back a transaction means undoing its effects. Think of it as being like the undo key in your editor: it lets you say, "Oops, that's not what I wanted," and get back to where you were before you started typing.

Rolling back

6.5 Using SQL in Programs

Every database I've ever used has a command-line interface, so you can throw SQL at it and have it send the results to standard output. To create the examples for this chapter, for instance, I used command lines like this:

```
sqlite example.db < xyz.sql | python showtable.py > xyz.txt
```

That's fine for simple stuff, but in more complex situations, you will want the database to hand the results directly to your program so that you don't have to parse its text output yourself. (Getting the results directly also gives you better control over error handling, since it means the database can throw an exception at your program.)

Just about every language in common use today lets programmers get at databases by making SQL queries through a bridging library. The grandmother of these libraries is ODBC, which stands for Open DataBase Connectivity. Its most widely used descendent today, JDBC, gives Java programmers a more-or-less uniform way to talk to Oracle, DB2, Microsoft Access, MySQL, PostgreSQL, SQLite, and dozens of other databases. Python's DB-API does the same for Python, Perl's DBI does it for Perl, and so on.

Here's a short example that shows how to get the names of all the consultants in Python:

```python
import sys, sqlite
connection = sqlite.connect("example.db")
cursor = connection.cursor()
cursor.execute("SELECT Person.FirstName, Person.LastName FROM Person;")
results = cursor.fetchall()
for r in results:
    print r
cursor.close()
connection.close()
```

cursor

The program starts by connecting to the database; typically, this requires extra parameters, such as a user name and password. It then creates a *cursor*, which, like the cursor in an editor, is simply a pointer to a particular database record. The program points the cursor at some data by having the database execute a query; cursor.fetchall() then loads the results of that query into memory for printing. Finally, the cursor and the connection are closed (just as a file would be after its contents had been read).

Simple, right? Not quite—I've left a couple of important things out. First, reading everything in at once with fetchall() is fine for small data sets (up to a few thousand records), but if there could be millions of records, you should use fetchone(). As the name suggests, this gets the next record from the result set, or *None* if there are no more records.

```
Line 1    import java.sql.*;

   -      class UpdatePerson {

   5          public static final String CHANGE = \
   -              "UPDATE Person" +
   -              " SET Person.FirstName = \"Charles\"" +
   -              " WHERE (Person.EmpId = 4004);";

   10          public static final String QUERY = \
   -              "SELECT Person.FirstName, Person.LastName FROM Person;";

   -          public static void main(String argv[]) {

   15              try {
   -                  Class.forName("sqlite.JdbcDriver");
   -                  Connection con =
   -                      DriverManager.getConnection("jdbc:sqlite:example",
   -                                                  "admin", "pragmatic");
   20
   -                  Statement stmt = con.createStatement();
   -                  stmt.executeQuery(CHANGE);
   -                  con.commit();

   25                  ResultSet rs = stmt.executeQuery(QUERY);
   -                  while (rs.next()) {
   -                      String firstName = rs.getString(1);
   -                      String lastName = rs.getString(2);
   -                      System.out.println(lastName + ", " + firstName);
   30                  }

   -                  stmt.close();
   -                  con.close();
   -              }
   35
   -              catch (ClassNotFoundException ex) {
   -                  System.out.println(ex);
   -              }

   40              catch (SQLException ex) {
   -                  System.err.println(ex);
   -                  con.rollback();
   -              }
   -          }
   45      }
```

Figure 6.6: Example JDBC Program

Second, this program doesn't handle errors. In the real world, you always have to worry about things going wrong, particularly when you're inserting data rather than reading it.[11]

Figure 6.6 shows a Java program that takes errors into account. It connects to

---

[11]There's always the possibility that someone else will have updated the database between the time you decided what to change and the time you told the database to make that change.

the database by loading the database's JDBC driver (line 16) and then opening a connection by URL (line 17). It then creates a statement to update a consultant's name, executes it, and shows what the table contains (lines 21 to 30). If the database driver can't be found, it prints out an error message (line 36). More important, if the *UPDATE* statement fails, it catches the *SQLException* and rolls back the transaction (line 40) so that any changes that may have occurred are thrown away.

Objects and Tables

Just before we close, it's worth spending a moment talking about some of the problems that come up when you try to connect an object-oriented program to a relational database. It's common to think of a table's columns as being like a record type definition in a programming language and of each row of the table as being an instance of that type. As soon as you add inheritance to the mix, though, the analogy breaks down. For example, suppose you have the following simple class hierarchy:

```
class Shape {
    . . .
    protected float centerX, centerY;
}
class Circle extends Shape {
    . . .
    protected float radius;
}
class Rectangle extends Shape {
    . . .
    protected float sizeX, sizeY;
}
```

You can represent the relationships between these classes in database tables in three different ways:

- ignore inheritance, and represent each class with a table of its own;
- store common data members in one table, and then add more information in separate tables; or
- store all objects in one big table, and just leave out values for members that don't exist.

Unfortunately, all three are flawed. As you can see from Figure 6.7 on the next page, they all make work for data crunching programs: you either have to combine information from several tables in order to construct a single object or throw away information that doesn't apply to your particular object's class when building it.

This mismatch and various ways to work around it are discussed in detail on the

①

Circle

centerX	centerY	radius
0.4	0.5	0.6
0.7	0.8	0.9

Rectangle

centerX	centerY	sizeX	sizeY
1.1	1.2	1.3	1.4
2.1	2.2	2.3	2.4

②

Shape

id	centerY	centerY
9027	0.4	0.5
9139	0.7	0.8
8660	1.1	1.2
8685	2.1	2.2

Circle

id	radius
9027	0.6
9139	0.9

Rectangle

id	sizeX	sizeY
8660	1.3	1.4
8685	2.3	2.4

③

Shape

type	centerY	centerY	radius	sizeX	sizeY
Circle	0.4	0.5	0.6		
Circle	0.7	0.8	0.9		
Rectangle	1.1	1.2		1.3	1.4
Rectangle	2.1	2.2		2.3	2.4

Figure 6.7: OBJECT/RELATIONAL MAPPING

web[12] and in [Amb03]. Object/relational mapping tools, like Hibernate for Java[13] and SQLObject for Python[14] can manage some of this complexity for you but are outside the scope of this book.

6.6 Summary

I'll close this chapter with a confession: I came to database programming late in life. Like many of my colleagues, I managed just fine with flat text files, thank you, until XML came along, and then I started putting everything in angle brackets. Databases? Databases were for banks and government work; databases were for people who didn't understanding that data is for grepping.[15]

Two things opened my eyes. One was building my first bigger-than-a-breadbox web site. XML was fine for storing information, but after a month or so, I realized that I was writing a *lot* of code to search it—code that could be replaced with just a few lines of SQL. Hmm...

The second thing that finally made me learn how to work with relational databases was SQLite (`http://www.sqlite.org`). It was so small that it didn't even have an installer: it was just a single program, no bigger than grep or find and no harder to use.

So, while they're still relatively fresh in my mind, here are a few key points about working with relational data:

- Every database uses its own dialect of SQL, so make sure you check the details of the one you're using.
- Don't try to cram everything into a single table. Every table should record exactly one relationship; use joins to connect the dots when you need to.
- Always keep SQL's evaluation model in mind: every query constructs a cross product, filters the resulting rows according to the condition in the *WHERE* and then keeps the values in the columns named in the *SELECT*.
- Use aliases and views to simplify your queries.
- Use nested queries and negation to select records that *don't* have certain properties; use aggregation functions to combine information from multiple records.
- Remember that real data is never complete, so keep an eye out for nulls.
- Use transactions when adding, modifying, or deleting records.

---

[12]`http://www.agiledata.org/essays/impedanceMismatch.html`
[13]`http://www.hibernate.org`
[14]`http://www.sqlobject.org`
[15]See Section 3.6, *Grep*, on page 71.

## Chapter 7

Horseshoe Nails

There's an old children's rhyme that goes

> For want of a nail the shoe was lost.
> For want of a shoe the horse was lost.
> For want of a horse the rider was lost.
> For want of a rider the battle was lost.
> For want of a battle the kingdom was lost.
> And all for the want of a horseshoe nail.

In honor of that rhyme, engineers sometimes use the term *horseshoe nails* to refer to those apparently trivial things that can bring the whole system crashing down when they go wrong.

This chapter discusses some of the horseshoe nails of data crunching. No matter what tools you're crunching data with, these topics come up again and again.

7.1   Unit Testing

When historians of the future come to write the annals of our times, they—sorry, that was a bit pretentious. Let me try again....

In retrospect, the real revolution in programming in the last decade hasn't been the shift to distributed net-based systems. Instead, it has been the spread of test-driven development. Whether you buy into agile methodologies like Extreme Programming or not, you can't deny that

- tools like the JUnit testing framework have made testing easier than ever before;

- as a result, more programmers are writing and running tests on a daily (or even hourly) basis;

- the software they're creating is thereby more reliable than it would otherwise have been; and

- the software they're creating is also cleaner, since unit testing forces programmers to modularize more and makes refactoring easier and safer.

It's tempting to skip testing when crunching data, especially if the crunching in question has to be done only once (e.g., to reformat a legacy data file). However, experience has taught me that testing doesn't just find errors in my programs: it also keeps me honest. If I know that I'm going to write a few tests for a piece of code, I'm more likely to write the code itself cleanly and correctly.

That said, I usually test data crunching programs less rigorously than production code. When I'm working on the latter, I write unit tests to make sure that each method does what it's supposed to. When this proves difficult, I refactor my code to make testing easier, since something that's hard to test will almost always be hard to upgrade or replace in future.

When I'm writing a data crunching program, on the other hand, I usually concentrate on end-to-end functional testing; in other words, I feed it some data and check the results. I only start writing separate unit tests for the input, processing, and output when things go so badly wrong that I can't fix them in five minutes or less. Some of my colleagues[1] believe that this is terribly misguided and that I'm putting my soul in jeopardy by not always writing unit tests up front, but it seems to work for me. (That said, the older I get, the more preemptive testing I do....)

The first step in testing a data crunching program is deciding how you're going to do it. Broadly speaking, the two options are sampling and auditing, or comparing your program's output to examples you know are correct. If you choose the latter, you can do the comparison externally using tools like diff, or use string I/O to construct self-contained test suites for frameworks like JUnit. The following three sections look at each option in turn.

Sampling and Auditing

During rush hour in Toronto, I can get on the street car by either the front or the rear doors. I'm supposed to board at the rear only if I have a monthly pass or a transfer from the subway or a bus. No one is there to check—it would be too expensive to put two conductors on every car. Every once in a while, though, inspectors board the trolleys and check that everyone has some proof of payment. Anyone who doesn't is fined on the spot; penalties are steep enough that almost everyone buys a ticket rather than take the risk.

---

[1]Including the editors of this series.

Purists sometimes turn their noses up at random sampling, since it isn't guaranteed to catch mistakes, but sampling is often the most cost-effective way to find out if a data crunching program is working correctly. For example, suppose that you're processing expense claims from customer support engineers. Your input is three files. The first holds information about employees:

```
# NAME           EMAIL            ID
Hunt, Dave       dave             3001
Thomas, Andy     andy             3002
Wilson, Greg     gvwilson         4001
```

The second holds information about their expenses:

```
# ID          DATE          CURRENCY   AMOUNT   REASON
gvwilson      2004-11-18    CDN        48.22    books
andy          2004-12-09    US         149.95   printer/scanner
andy          2004-12-10    US         79.95    toner
andy          2004-12-20    US         79.95    toner
gvwilson      2004-12-25    CDN        127.05   phone charges
andy          2005-01-03    US         79.95    toner
```

and the third is a currency conversion table:

```
# FROM        TO            RATE
CDN           US            0.7954
```

You're supposed to produce a file with a running total of each employee's expenses, in American dollars, sorted by employee name and date:

```
# NAME           DATE          TOTAL
Wilson, Greg     2004-11-18    38.35
                 2004-12-25    139.40
Thomas, Andy     2004-12-09    149.95
                 2004-12-10    229.90
                 2004-12-20    308.85
                 2005-01-03    389.80
```

In order to make sure that the little Python program you wrote is working, you could choose twenty lines of input at random, run it through your program, and check the output by hand. If you do this, it's important that you save the input, or have some way to reselect exactly the same values, so that if you find any problems, you can rerun your program on exactly the same test data in order to check your fixes. The reason is that if you select a different input set for checking, it may not tickle the original error, so you may not be able to tell whether your fix is correct.

You should also select your test input randomly, rather than using a regular rule like "every 100th line." Data often contains patterns; if your tests happen to resonate with those patterns, they can skip over every input record of a certain kind and leave some pretty nasty bugs in your program.

This may sound far-fetched, but it comes up surprisingly often in practice. For example, I once had to reformat some data from a set of experiments that measured how well firefighters' helmets withstood impact shocks (like falling bricks) after varying degrees of thermal degradation (what you and I would call melting). In order to test my program, I put every *hundred*th input record in a separate file and then ran my cruncher on that and drew a graph. Everything looked fine—at first.

What I didn't know was that the experiments had been done in fixed-size batches: ten different weights were dropped on each helmet after it had been been heated to one of ten different temperatures. As a result, I was sampling only the data for test #1 on each helmet. This meant that all of my test data had been entered by the same guy. Unfortunately, the other two technicians working on the problem entered their data differently....

So, how can you select random input? The simplest way is to read the input as normal and then use the ratio between the number of records you have and the number you want as the probability of keeping any particular record. You can then use your favorite random number generator to decide which records to keep. For example, here's a function that selects approximately N lines from a list at random:

```python
def keepN(lines, N):
    # Make sure random number generation is reproducible.
    random.seed(12345213)

    # If not enough data, return what's there.
    if (not lines) or (len(lines) <= N):
        return lines[:]

    # Probability of keeping any line.
    prob = float(N) / len(lines)

    # Select.
    result = []
    for l in lines:
        if random.random() < prob:
            result.append(l)

    return result
```

This is also another good argument in favor of writing data crunching programs as a series of filter functions: the random selector is just another filter that may or may not be run after reading the initial data.

Diff

Checking a program's output by hand over and over again is so tedious and error-prone that most of us would rather skip testing than do it. One way to ease the tedium is to automate the checking using diff, a tool that prints out the differences between two text files.[2]

---

[2]You can also use Python's difflib library or similar libraries in other languages.

For instance, if `a.txt` contains

```
one
two
three
four
```

and `b.txt` contains

```
two
three
three
five
```

then `diff a.txt b.txt` prints out

```
1d0
< one
4c3,4
< four
---
> three
> five
```

The alphanumeric codes `1d0` and `4c3,4` are actually commands for an editor that hasn't been used by anyone except die-hard Unix nerds in twenty-five years. Each introduces a section showing a difference between the two files: < indicates lines from the first one, and > indicates lines from the second.

So, suppose you know what output your data crunching program is supposed to produce for some test input data. If you put that output in a file called expected.txt, you can run your cruncher and compare its actual output to what you expected in a single step, like this:

```
crunch < input | diff - expected.txt
```

The `-` argument to diff makes it read one set of data from standard input, rather than a file. If crunch's output is identical to what's in expected.txt, the command above won't print anything at all. If there are differences, on the other hand, diff will show you where they are. You can then patch your cruncher and rerun your test.[3]

If your shell has a "repeat previous command" feature (and they all do these days), that's enough—until you're dragged away to put out another fire and can't get back to processing expense claims for a week. If you had built up a dozen or more test cases, the odds are pretty long that you won't remember all of them.

For this reason, whenever I'm doing anything that will take more than five minutes to complete, I (almost) always start by writing a little Makefile. This Makefile doesn't recompile anything (unless I'm using Java or some other sturdy language).

---

[3]If diff's output is too hard to read, you can use a GUI tool such as windiff, xdiff, or meld.

Make

Make is one of the most widely used programming tools in the world. It was invented by Stuart Feldman at Bell Labs; he noticed that everyone wrote the same kind of shell script over and over again to recompile their programs, and decided that a specialized tool would make everyone's life easier. (Feldman went on to become a vice president of IBM, which shows you how far a good tool can take you.)

Like many classic Unix tools, Make's configuration files (called Makefiles) are written in an idiosyncratic syntax. As Make has grown more complex over the years, so too have Makefiles: real ones now contain function calls, conditionals, and many other features.

A Makefile contains zero or more rules, each of which has a head and a body. The head specifies a dependency between one or more *targets* and zero or more *prerequisites*. Targets and prerequisites are typically filenames, such as object files, HTML pages, and so on. Targets and prerequisites are separated from one another by spaces, and the set of targets is separated from the prerequisites by a single colon.

The body specifies zero or more *actions*, which are shell commands for bringing the target up to date. If any of the rule's prerequisites are newer than the target, Make executes the actions. In this example, the program xyz is built from the source file xyz.c, and the header file defs.h.

```
xyz : xyz.c defs.h
        cc -o xyz xyz.c
```

Here, xyz is the target, xyz.c and defs.h are the prerequisites, and the body contains a single action. A more complex example is

```
# Build the program
xyz xyz.lst : xyz.o util.o
        cc -WZall -o xyz xyz.o util.o
# Build the objects
xyz.o : xyz.c defs.h
        cc -c xyz.c
util.o : util.c defs.h
        cc -c util.c
# Clean up
clean :
        rm -f xyz xyz.lst *.o *~
```

The most important feature of Make is that it keeps track of dependencies *between* rules: if util.c changes, Make recompiles util.o, notices that util.o is now newer than xyz and xyz.lst, and rebuilds those two files. Similarly, if you tell Make that certain tests depend on certain files, then when those files change, Make will automatically rerun exactly the right set of tests.

Instead, each of its rules reruns one of my tests, while another rule runs *all* of my tests, in order. An example is

```
all : t_empty t_single t_dup t_long t_name t_currency
t_empty :
        python crunch.py < empty-input.txt | diff - empty-output.txt
t_single :
        python crunch.py < single-input.txt | diff - single-output.txt
    :           :             :
```

If I type make, Make runs each of my tests for me. If everything is working as it should, all I'll see is the commands echoed to the screen one after another. If I see any diff output, I know that something has gone wrong, and I can go and fix it.

String I/O

If I'm going to go to the trouble of putting tests in a Makefile, I might as well go one step further and write proper unit tests. In fact, if I'm serious about having my data crunching program do the right thing, I should write those tests *before* I start writing the cruncher. This forces me to think through what I'm supposed to do to the data, rather than retrofitting my expectations around the code I've already written. It also gives me a concrete goal to work toward: as soon as all my tests run, I can stop fiddling with the program and go on to my next task.

These days, the standard way to write unit tests is to use a framework like JUnit (for Java) or one of its clones like unittest (for Python), NUnit (for .NET), or Test::Unit (for Ruby). Each framework has its own quirks but typically works as follows:

- Derive a class from a base class provided by the framework (in Java, the base class is junit.framework.TestCase).

- Add one method to that class for each test you want to run. These methods must follow a few simple rules—for example, they must take no arguments, they must return nothing, and their names must start with the letters *test*— but other than that, they can do whatever they want.

- Inside each method, the programmer creates data structures, calls functions, and so on, and then checks the results using special assertion methods provided by the framework. If the assertions pass, the framework adds one to the count of successful tests. If any of the assertions fail, or if something goes wrong inside the test itself, the framework catches and reports the error.

This pattern works well when the tests are self-contained, but data crunching programs almost always need external data as input and are expected to produce

---

Test-Driven Development

One of the core practices of Extreme Programming is *test-driven development* (TDD), which tells programmers to write their test cases *before* they write their code. While this seems backward, it has several benefits:

- It forces you to think about exactly what your code is going to do, before you write it.

- It gives you goalposts to aim for. When all the tests pass, you're done.

- It keeps you honest by making it harder to change the problem definition (consciously or unconsciously) in order to avoid difficult coding.

- It means you actually *do* write tests.

TDD is a great way to approach any data crunching problem that can't be solved with a simple command-line pipe. Pick a few samples of input (or make them up), figure out what the output should be, stick them side by side in a Makefile or some other testing harness, and then write your cruncher. I promise, it'll be faster than writing the cruncher and then tweaking it over and over again to eliminate bugs.

(For more on test-driven development, see (Bec02).)

---

external data (such as new files) as output. You *can* put the input and expected output data in files and have your unit tests read and diff them, but there's a better way.

The trick is that almost every language in use today has some way of treating a string as a file. In C++, the class that does this is called `stringstream`; in Python, it's `StringIO` (and its faster cousin, `cStringIO`). Java provides a pair of classes called `StringReader` and `StringWriter`, .NET gives you `MemoryStream`, and so on. In each case, the string I/O class can be used in place of a "real" file, causing the program to read from, or write to, a buffer in memory. Here's a simple example in Python:

```python
import cStringIO

data = """This is
a multi-line string
but we will read it
as if it were
a file."""
input = cStringIO.StringIO(data)
for line in input:
    print len(line)
input.close()
```

Its output is

```
8
20
20
14
7
```

Suppose we're writing a data crunching program called crunch.py that's supposed to read a single file from standard input, transform that data in some way, and write the result to standard ouptut. We can structure crunch.py like this:

```python
# Entry point for processing.
def doTheWork(input, output):
    :   :   :
    read from input and write to output
    :   :   :
# Main driver.
if __name__ == "__main__":
    import sys
    doTheWork(sys.stdin, sys.stdout)
```

Now, create a second program called testcrunch.py, and define a test class called Tests. Each test method in the class passes two strings, containing input and expected output, to a utility method called runTheTest(). (I usually just copy and paste some of my actual input into the test program to create the input strings.) This method wraps the input to create a stream-like object, then creates another stream-like object to capture the output of processing, and compares the actual and expected output:

```python
import unittest, cStringIO
from crunch import doTheWork

class Tests(unittest.TestCase):
    def testEmpty():
        input = ""
        output = ""
        runTheTest(input, output)

    def testDouble():
        # Use Python's multi-line strings for this test.
        input = """\
first
second
"""

        output = """\
f
s
"""

        runTheTest(input, output)

    def runTheTest(input, expected):
        inputStream = cStringIO.StringIO(input)
        actual = cStringIO.StringIO()
        doTheWork(inputStream, actual)
        self.assertEqual(actual.getvalue(), expected)

unittest.main()
```

Voila! When we run testcrunch.py, Python runs each of our tests for us, telling us how many passed and which ones failed (if any).

Writing unit tests for a data crunching program may seem like more trouble than it's worth. As I said earlier, though, writing tests before you code is a great way to force yourself to think through the permutations, combinations, and corner cases that lurk inside every nontrivial programming problem (and many of the trivial ones as well). It's also the best way to make sure that as you fix one bug, you don't (re)introduce another.

7.2 Encoding and Decoding

We've run into escape sequences several times already in this book. In C and its offspring, characters that can't be put directly into strings, like newlines and bells, can be written as two-character sequences, where the first character is a backslash and the second specifies which special character is needed. In XML, escape sequences start with an ampersand and end with a semicolon. The characters in between can be either an abbreviated name like *lt* (for "less than", or <) or *ccedil* (for a lower-case *c* with a cedilla, ç).

encoding   Escape sequences are just one kind of *encoding*. Many other kinds are often used to represent data that would otherwise be difficult to type in or interpret. The following sections look at two common encodings, explain when and why they're used, and show how to handle them.

The most important rule to keep in mind when dealing with encoded data is this: don't write code to handle it yourself unless you absolutely have to do so. Almost every language provides library functions to deal with every encoding you're likely to encounter in the wild. If Google can't find them, mail one of the language's mailing lists; if that doesn't work, mail me, or stand on a street corner holding up a sign with your question on it. Do *not* write encoding and decoding routines for HTML escapes, URLs, and the like yourself—the only thing you can do that the library doesn't is make mistakes.

URL Encoding

According to RFC 1738, which is the official spec for URLs, "Only alphanumerics [0-9a-zA-Z], the special characters $-_.+!*'(),, and reserved characters used for their reserved purposes may be used unencoded within a URL." The "reserved characters" include

```
$  &  +  ,  /  :  ;  =  ?  @
```

"Reserved purposes" means that the characters indicate something special when they appear in a URL. For example, if values are being submitted as part of the

URL, they are separated from the path by ?, from each other by &, and from parameter names by =, like this:

```
http://www.pragprog.com/submit.cgi?name=gvwilson&purpose=example
```

So, how do you send a value that includes one of the special characters? The answer is that you use its two-digit hexadecimal code instead of the character itself, with a % in front of it to signal that it has been escaped. The hex codes for the special characters listed above are

$	%24	:	%3A
&	%26	;	%3B
+	%2B	=	%3D
,	%2C	?	%3F
/	%2F	@	%40

In addition, some other characters ought to be encoded, even though the standard doesn't strictly call for it, since they can confuse some browsers and servers if they aren't. The most common of these is the space character, whose code is %20; the percent sign itself is usually also encoded, as %25.

So, suppose you have a base URL and a list of key/value pairs. You want to create a URL, and you're bound and determined to ignore my earlier advice about using Python's urllib.urlencode() and its peers in other languages. What should you do? You should go back and reread my advice, that's what you should do.

Oh, you're still here? OK, if you insist...Here's a simple function to URL encode the values you want to submit and concatenate them onto the base URL:

```
Special = ("%", " ", "$", "&", "+", ",",
           "/", ":", ";", "=", "?", "@")
def encodeString(str):
    for c in Special:
        v = "%" + "%02X" % ord(c)
        str = str.replace(c, v)
    return str
def encode(baseUrl, extras):
    result = baseUrl
    sep = "?"
    for (key, value) in extras:
        key = encodeString(key)
        value = encodeString(value)
        result = result + sep + key + "=" + value
        sep = "&"
    return result
```

Code to break a URL into pieces, and decode each piece, is just as easy to write—which is a shame, because you shouldn't be doing it. You should be using the library routines.

Base-64 Encoding

base64

After URL encoding, the most common encoding format for data on the web is probably *base64*. It was originally developed as a safe way to include binary data (i.e., data that might include bytes that corresponded to ASCII control codes) in email, but is now often used to store binary data in XML documents.

Lots of libraries do base-64 encoding; as always, using one of those will save you a lot of time and mistakes. Just so you understand what they do, here are the rules they follow.

To convert an arbitrary sequence of bytes to base-64, put the first byte in the most significant 8 bits of a 24-bit buffer, the second byte in the middle 8 bits, and the third byte in the least significant 8 bits. Next, break that 24-bit buffer into four 6-bit chunks. Each chunk represents one of the 64 values in the range 0...63 (i.e., 2^6-1). Use those values as indices into the following character array:

```
ABCDEFGHIJKLMNOPQRSTUVWXYZabcdefghijklmnopqrstuvwxyz0123456789+/
```

If there were only one or two input bytes, pad the output with one or two equals signs, so that the decoder won't accidentally add extra bits to the reconstructed data. The result is four bytes for each three bytes of input but can safely be included in just about any text file you can think of.

This process isn't as arbitrary as it seems. Where base-16 (hexadecimal) adds six new "digits" A–F to the traditional 0–9, base-64 encoding adds 54 new digits (the alphabetic characters +, and /). This would be easier to see if 0–9 were at the front of the encoding array, but the principle remains: break the data into 6-bit chunks, and represent each in a base-64 numerical system (I've searched for an explanation of why they aren't but haven't turned anything up. I'd enjoy hearing from any reader who knows the reason).

7.3 Floating-Point Arithmetic

Section 5.1, *Numbers*, on page 118 discussed the problem of integer overflow. Well, floating-point numbers can overflow too. They can also underflow, and sometimes, adding and subtracting has no effect.

To see why, let's take a look at a very simpleminded 5-bit floating-point format. The first three bits are the fractional part, or *mantissa*, and the last two are the exponent (Figure 7.1 on the facing page). The mantissa is unsigned, so its value can range from 0 to 7. The exponent, on the other hand, uses two's complement; its possible values are 0, 1, –1, and –2, which represent 1 (2^0), 2 (2^1), $\frac{1}{2}$ (2^{-1}), and $\frac{1}{4}$ (2^{-2}) respectively. Put the two parts together, and we can represent the following unique values:

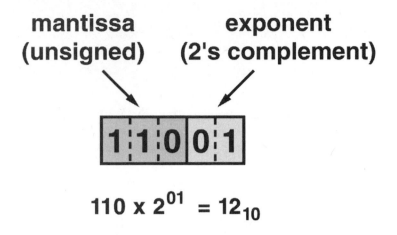

$$110 \times 2^{01} = 12_{10}$$

Figure 7.1: SIMPLE FLOATING-POINT REPRESENTATION

		Mantissa							
		000	001	010	011	100	101	110	111
	$2^0 = 1$ **00**	0	1	2	3	4	5	6	7
	$2^1 = 2$ **01**					8	10	12	14
	$2^{-1} = \frac{1}{2}$ **10**		1/2		3/2		5/2		7/2
	$2^{-2} = \frac{1}{4}$ **11**		1/4		3/4		5/4		7/4

Figure 7.2 on the next page shows how these values are distributed. Real floating-point representations, like the IEEE-754 standard, use some clever tricks to get more even coverage without duplicating as many values as this scheme. This webpage[4] will tell you everything you need to know for day-to-day work; if you really, really want more detail, visit the IEEE's web site.[5]

Now, suppose you have 7 (which is represented as 11100), and you add $\frac{1}{4}$ (00111) to it. The answer should be $\frac{29}{4}$, but that's not one of the values this scheme can represent. This means that if we do

```
int x = 7;
for (int i=0; i<1000000; ++i) {
    x = x + 0.25;
}
```

---

[4]http://stevehollasch.com/cgindex/coding/ieeefloat.html
[5]http://grouper.ieee.org/groups/754/

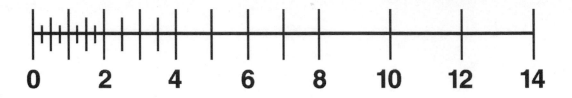

Figure 7.2: SIMPLE FLOATING-POINT NUMBER LINE

Roundoff Isn't Random

A lot of programmers seem to think that floating-point roundoff is some kind of statistically random process. It isn't: every time you do a calculation with x and y, you'll get exactly the same answer (unless a cosmic ray happens to hit your processor at the wrong nanosecond). Doing the same calculation over three times, and taking the average, is completely pointless, and a sign that you should read sidebars in books like this more closely.

---

x will still be 7 at the end. The same thing will happen if we add $\frac{3}{4}$ to 12, and so on; it's another manifestation of Spolsky's Law of Leaky Abstractions (Section 5.4, *Summary*, on page 136).

This isn't a clever trick; it happens with *every* finite-sized representation of real numbers. If you have a C++ compiler handy, try compiling and running this little code fragment:

```
double x = 100.0;
double y = 95.0;
if (y == (x * (y / x))) {
   cout << "Equal" << endl;
} else {
   cout << "Unequal" << endl;
}
```

On some machines, this prints out *Unequal*, because 0.95 can't be represented exactly, even in the 64 bits used to store a *double*. It might be something like 0.94999999999 or 0.9500000001; either way, when you multiply it by 100.0, the answer is *not* the 95.0 you started with.

Entire books—no, entire libraries—have been written about how to cope with these issues. Most of the answers are out of our scope, but as a rule

- Do not use == when comparing floating-point numbers. Instead, check whether the difference between them is less than some very small value (usually called *epsilon*, in honor of first-year calculus courses).

- When adding or subtracting lists of values, sort them first and then work from smallest (in absolute value) to largest.[6]

- If your problems are such that you need to pay attention to either of the previous two rules, go and read up on numerical programming. Yes, it's mind-numbing (and I'm speaking as someone who spent ten years programming for physicists and enjoyed most of it), but what's more important: your sanity or getting the right answer?

7.4 Dates and Times

Pop quiz: what is the extra day in a leap year? If you said February 29, you're wrong—it's actually February 24, at least from the point of view of feast days in the Christian calendar. And did you know that when someone refers to 15 March 429 BC, they're almost certainly using the Julian calendar, rather than the more modern Gregorian calendar that English-speaking countries switched to in 1752? In that year, September 2 was immediately followed by September 14, in order to get the calendar back in sync with the seasons.[7]

Of course, if you're in France, the switch took place in 1582. (At least, that's when most of modern France switched over; Alsace and Lorraine switched in 1682 and 1760, respectively.) And don't get me started on Sweden. For what probably seemed like good reasons at the time, the Swedes decided to make the change gradually between 1700 and 1740. Never mind the fact that this put them out of sync with the entire planet for forty years (which was literally a lifetime in those days): they mistakenly counted 1704 and 1708 as leap years and then decided to abandon the transition and go back to the Julian calendar until 1753.

Other than tax law, calendrical calculations are the only field that can challenge programming for seemingly arbitrary rules. In a well-designed cosmos, years would be an integral number of days long, and the moon would go around the Earth exactly twelve times every year. The Earth itself would be flat, too, so that we wouldn't need those pesky time zones. (Either that, or we'd persuade everyone

---

[6]In most cases, you can do even better than this by calculating partial sums and then adding them, since the partial sums are more likely to be close to one another in magnitude than the original values.

[7]The riots that ensued were due in part to the fact that many landlords charged a full month's rent.

living east and west of Greenwich to get up really, really early in the morning or sleep in until the middle of the afternoon.) Until we get there, though, we're stuck with writing software to handle the current mishmash of leap seconds, daylight saving time, and all the rest.

Let's get some definitions out of the way first:

- *Coordinated Universal Time*, or *UTC*, is the standard clock in terms of which all others are defined. Its predecessor was Greenwich Mean Time, or *GMT*.

instant

- An *instant* is a particular moment in time, i.e., a particular time of a particular day. While most Americans write dates as month-day-year, the standard is actually year-month-day (just as you'd write miles-feet-inches, not feet-inches-miles). My birthday, for example, is 1963-01-25 (January 25, 1963). Instants cannot be added to one another, but you can subtract one from another to get...

duration

- A *duration*, which is a length of time like two years, or 39.357 milliseconds. Durations are always the same length, which means that there's no duration corresponding to "one month" (since different months have different lengths). Every different language and database system has its own way to represent such "human-oriented" durations.

If you're a standards geek, you write instants according to the ISO-8601 standards, which specifies that the moment of my birth was 19630125T13:00:00 (i.e., 1:00 p.m. UTC on January 25, 1963, or five o'clock in the morning in British Columbia). When you're crunching data, though, you have to worry about dozens of other formats: the American month-day-year, the British day-month-year, two-digit as well as four-digit years, and so on. Good documentation is your friend here; without it, it's impossible to tell whether 05-01-88 is the fifth of January or the first of May (unless you have other records available that contain 07-29-89, in which case you can make an educated guess and cross your fingers).

Input and Output

Many people use regular expressions to parse dates and print them by formatting strings. This is almost always the wrong thing to do, since (a) most languages provide library routines to do the work for you, and (b) checking that what you've parsed is legal is a headache. (Quick, did you remember to allow for February 29? But not in years divisible by 100, unless the year is also divisible by 400?) In Java, the right way to parse dates is to use DateFormat.parse(), which takes a `String` as input, and either returns a valid `Date` object or throws a *ParseException*. If you're working in Python, there's time.strptime(); in Perl, there's Time::ParseDate(), and so on.

Outputting times is easy too. The grandaddy of 'em all is C's strftime(), which takes a format string and a time and writes a formatted representation of that time into a character buffer. Most agile languages, and many sturdy ones, have simply followed C's conventions. In Python, for example, the datetime object has a method called strftime(), which takes a format string as an argument and produces a string as output. The format characters allowed are

%a   Abbreviated weekday name.
%A   Full weekday name.
%b   Abbreviated month name.
%B   Full month name.
%c   Colloquial date and time representation.
%d   Day of the month as a decimal number [01,31].
%H   Hour (24-hour clock) as a decimal number [00,23].
%I   Hour (12-hour clock) as a decimal number [01,12].
%j   Day of the year as a decimal number [001,366].
%m   Month as a decimal number [01,12].
%M   Minute as a decimal number [00,59].
%p   Either AM or PM.
%S   Second as a decimal number [00,61] (includes leap seconds).
%U   Week number of the year as a decimal number [00,53].
%w   Weekday as a decimal number [0(Sunday),6].
%W   Week number of the year as a decimal number [00,53].
%x   Colloquial date representation.
%X   Colloquial time representation.
%y   Year without century as a decimal number [00,99].
%Y   Year with century as a decimal number.
%Z   Time zone name.
%%   A literal % character.

For example, here's a program to print today's date in the format most often used in email, in the format that Python thinks we use here in Ontario, and in ISO-8601:

```
import datetime
Formats = [
    "%a, %d %b %Y %H:%M:%S %Z",
    "%c",
    "%Y%m%dT%H:%M:%S"
]
t = datetime.datetime.today()
for f in Formats:
    print t.strftime(f)
```

Its output on Monday, November 22, 2004 is

```
Mon, 22 Nov 2004 17:48:41
11/22/04 17:48:41
20041122T17:48:41
```

Calculations

When you're crunching data, the two calculations you most commonly do with dates are comparing them to see which is earlier or later and adding or subtracting a duration to move forward or backward in time. The first is easy: Java's Date class, for example, has methods called before() and after(), which take another Date as an argument and return a Boolean to tell you whether the instant whose method you're calling is before or after the instant represented by the argument. Date also has a compareTo() method, which returns a negative value, zero, or a positive value if the date you're calling the method on is before, equal to, or after the date you pass in.

Moving around in time is more complicated. You don't actually have to slingshot around the sun, but you do have to worry about what happens when you add one month to January 31. Should the answer be February 28, February 29 (in a leap year), or one of the first two days of March?

The best way to find out what the libraries you're using think the answer is, is to write a small test program. This often takes less time than reading the documentation, since docs for anything to do with dates and times tend to be littered with *however* and *except*. Here's a Java program to step forward a month at a time from January 31, 2000:

```java
import java.util.Date;
import java.util.Calendar;
import java.util.GregorianCalendar;

public class Forward {
    public static void main(String[] args) {
        Calendar calendar = new GregorianCalendar(2000, 00, 31);
        for (int i=0; i<14; ++i) {
            Date d = calendar.getTime();
            System.out.println(d);
            calendar.add(Calendar.MONTH, 1);
        }
    }
}
```

Its output is

```
Mon Jan 31 00:00:00 EST 2000
Tue Feb 29 00:00:00 EST 2000
Wed Mar 29 00:00:00 EST 2000
Sat Apr 29 00:00:00 EDT 2000
Mon May 29 00:00:00 EDT 2000
Thu Jun 29 00:00:00 EDT 2000
Sat Jul 29 00:00:00 EDT 2000
Tue Aug 29 00:00:00 EDT 2000
Fri Sep 29 00:00:00 EDT 2000
```

```
Sun Oct 29 00:00:00 EDT 2000
Wed Nov 29 00:00:00 EST 2000
Fri Dec 29 00:00:00 EST 2000
Mon Jan 29 00:00:00 EST 2001
Wed Feb 28 00:00:00 EST 2001
```

Oh, and don't forget about daylight saving time—some days have 23 or 25 hours, just as some years have 366 days. And then there are leap seconds—since they are added to the calendar irregularly, on an as-needed basis, no off-the-shelf library (that I know of) takes them into account.

As with floating-point and binary data, calendrical calculation is an area where writing your own code is almost never the right answer. Java, Python, C#, and most other languages have good (if complicated) libraries these days for handling dates and times; if you really need to roll your own, read [RD01] very, very carefully first.

7.5 Summary

And that's it—that's everything you need to know to build little tools to move data around, reformat it, and extract information from it. To recap, here are the most important lessons to keep in mind:

- Start small. Build your data crunching tools in steps, and test each new feature as you add it.

- Don't write code unless you have to. You can do a lot with editor macros, and modern languages have libraries to handle regular expressions, XML, SQL, and every kind of binary data you're ever likely to see.

- Keep input, processing, and output separate.

- Make sure that the data you generate conforms to whatever rules it's supposed to, so that you don't create headaches for other people. Remember the Golden Rule: code unto others as you would have others code unto you.

- Remember that real data is never complete: not everyone has a last name or a cell phone number, so your crunching programs should complain (or fail) rather than inventing values that aren't there.

- Finally, always keep in mind that an hour of hard work can sometimes save you five minutes of thought.

Happy crunching!

Appendix A

Resources

A.1 Bibliography

[Amb03]   Scott Ambler. *Agile Database Techniques: Effective Strategies for the Agile Software Developer*. John Wiley & Sons, New York, NY, 2003.

[Bec02]   Kent Beck. *Test Driven Development: By Example*. Addison-Wesley, Reading, MA, 2002.

[Feh03]   Chris Fehily. *SQL: Visual QuickStart Guide*. Peachpit Press, Berkeley, CA, 2003.

[Fri97]   Jeffrey E. F. Friedl. *Mastering Regular Expressions*. O'Reilly & Associates, Inc, Sebastopol, CA, 1997.

[Har03]   Elliotte Rusty Harold. *Effective XML: 50 Specific Ways to Improve Your XML*. Addison-Wesley, Reading, MA, 2003.

[Her03]   Michael J. Hernandez. *Database Design for Mere Mortals*. Addison-Wesley, Reading, MA, second edition, 2003.

[HF04]   David Harel and Yishai Feldman. *Algorithmics: The Spirit of Computing*. Addison-Wesley, Reading, MA, third edition, 2004.

[HT00]   Andrew Hunt and David Thomas. *The Pragmatic Programmer: From Journeyman to Master*. Addison-Wesley, Reading, MA, 2000.

[KP78]   Brian W. Kernighan and P. J. Plauger. *The Elements of Programming Style*. McGraw-Hill, second edition, 1978.

[KP81]   Brian W. Kernighan and P. J. Plauger. *Software Tools in Pascal*. Addison-Wesley, 1981.

[KP84]   Brian W. Kernighan and Rob Pike. *The Unix Programming Environment*. Prentice Hall, 1984.

[KP99]   Brian W. Kernighan and Rob Pike. *The Practice of Programming*. Addison Wesley Longman, Reading, MA, 1999.

[KR98]   Brian W. Kernighan and Dennis Ritchie. *The C Programming Language*. Prentice Hall PTR, second edition, 1998.

[Man02]   Sal Mangano. *XSLT Cookbook*. O'Reilly & Associates, Inc, Sebastopol, CA, 2002.

[Par93]   C. Northcote Parkinson. *Parkinson's Law*. Buccaneer Books, 1993.

[RD01]   Edward M. Reingold and Nachum Dershowitz. *Calendrical Calculations: The Millenium Edition*. Cambridge University Press, New York, NY, 2001.

[Sed97]   Robert Sedgewick. *Algorithms in C, Parts 1-4*. Addison-Wesley, Reading, MA, 1997.

[Spo04]   Joel Spolsky. *Joel on Software: And on Diverse and Occasionally Related Matters That Will Prove of Interest to Software Developers, Designers, and Managers, and to Those Who, Whether by Good Fortune or Ill Luck, Work with Them in Some Capacity*. Apress, Berkeley, CA, 2004.

Index

Pragmatic Starter Kit Series

Version Control. **Unit Testing**. **Project Automation**. Three great titles, one objective. To get you up to speed with the essentials for successful project development. Keep your source under control, your bugs in check, and your process repeatable with these three concise, readable books from The Pragmatic Bookshelf.

• Keep your project assets safe—never lose a great idea • Know how to UNDO bad decisions—no matter when they were made • Learn how to share code safely, and work in parallel • See how to avoid costly code freezes • Manage 3rd party code • Understand how to go back in time, and work on previous versions.

Pragmatic Version Control using CVS
Dave Thomas and Andy Hunt
(176 pages) ISBN: 0-9745140-0-4. $29.95

Pragmatic Version Control using Subversion
Mike Mason
(224 pages) ISBN: 0-9745140-6-3. $29.95

• Write better code, faster • Discover the hiding places where bugs breed • Learn how to think of all the things that could go wrong • Test pieces of code without using the whole project • Use JUnit to simplify your test code • Test effectively with the whole team.

Pragmatic Unit Testing
Andy Hunt and Dave Thomas
(176 pages) ISBN: 0-9745140-1-2. $29.95
(Also available for C#, ISBN: 0-9745140-2-0)

• Common, freely available tools which automate build, test, and release procedures • Effective ways to keep on top of problems • Automate to create better code, and save time and money • Create and deploy releases easily and automatically • Have programs to monitor themselves and report problems.

Pragmatic Project Automation
Mike Clark
(176 pages) ISBN: 0-9745140-3-9. $29.95

Visit our secure online store: http://pragmaticprogrammer.com/catalog

Facets of Ruby Series

Learn how to use the popular Ruby programming language from the Pragmatic Programmers: your definitive source for reference and tutorials on the Ruby language and exciting new application development tools based on Ruby.

The *Facets of Ruby* series includes the definitive guide to Ruby, widely known as the PickAxe book. Upcoming titles in this series feature the *Ruby on Rails* web application framework and other exciting new technologies.

- The definitive guide for Ruby programmers.

- Up-to-date and expanded for Ruby version 1.8.

- Complete documentation of all built-in classes, modules, and methods.

- Complete descriptions of all of the ninety-eight standard libraries.

- 200+ pages of new content in this edition.

- Learn more about Ruby's web tools, unit testing, and programming philosophy.

Programming Ruby: The Pragmatic Programmer's Guide, 2nd Edition
Dave Thomas with Chad Fowler and Andy Hunt
(864 pages) ISBN: 0-9745140-5-5. $44.95

Visit our store at http://pragmaticprogrammer.com/catalog

The Pragmatic Bookshelf

The Pragmatic Starter Kit series: Three great titles, one objective. To get you up to speed with the essentials for successful project development. Keep your source under control, your bugs in check, and your process repeatable with these three concise, readable books.

Facets of Ruby series: Learn all about developing applications using the Ruby programming language, from the famous Pickaxe book to the latest books featuring Ruby On Rails.

The Pragmatic Bookshelf features books written by developers for developers. The titles continue the well-known Pragmatic Programmer style, and continue to garner awards and rave reviews. As development gets more and more difficult, the Pragmatic Programmers will be there with more titles and products to help programmers stay on top of their game.

Visit Us Online

Data Crunching Home Page
pragmaticprogrammer.com/titles/gwd
Source code from this book, errata, and other resources. Come give us feedback, too!

Register for Updates
pragmaticprogrammer.com/updates
Be notified when updates and new books become available.

Join the Community
pragmaticprogrammer.com/community
Read our weblogs, join our online discussions, participate in our mailing list, interact with our wiki, and benefit from the experience of other Pragmatic Programmers.

New and Noteworthy
pragmaticprogrammer.com/news
Check out the latest pragmatic developments in the news.

Save on the PDF

Save more than 60% on the PDF version of this book. Owning the paper version of this book entitles you to purchase the PDF version for only $7.50 (regularly $20). That's a saving of more than 60%. The PDF is great for carrying around on your laptop. It's hyperlinked, has color, and is fully searchable. Buy it now at pragmaticprogrammer.com/coupon

Contact Us

Phone Orders:	1-800-699-PROG (+1 919 847 3884)
Online Orders:	www.pragmaticprogrammer.com/catalog
Customer Service:	orders@pragmaticprogrammer.com
Non-English Versions:	translations@pragmaticprogrammer.com
Pragmatic Teaching:	academic@pragmaticprogrammer.com
Author Proposals:	proposals@pragmaticprogrammer.com